*How to Teach Adults
Without Really Suffering*

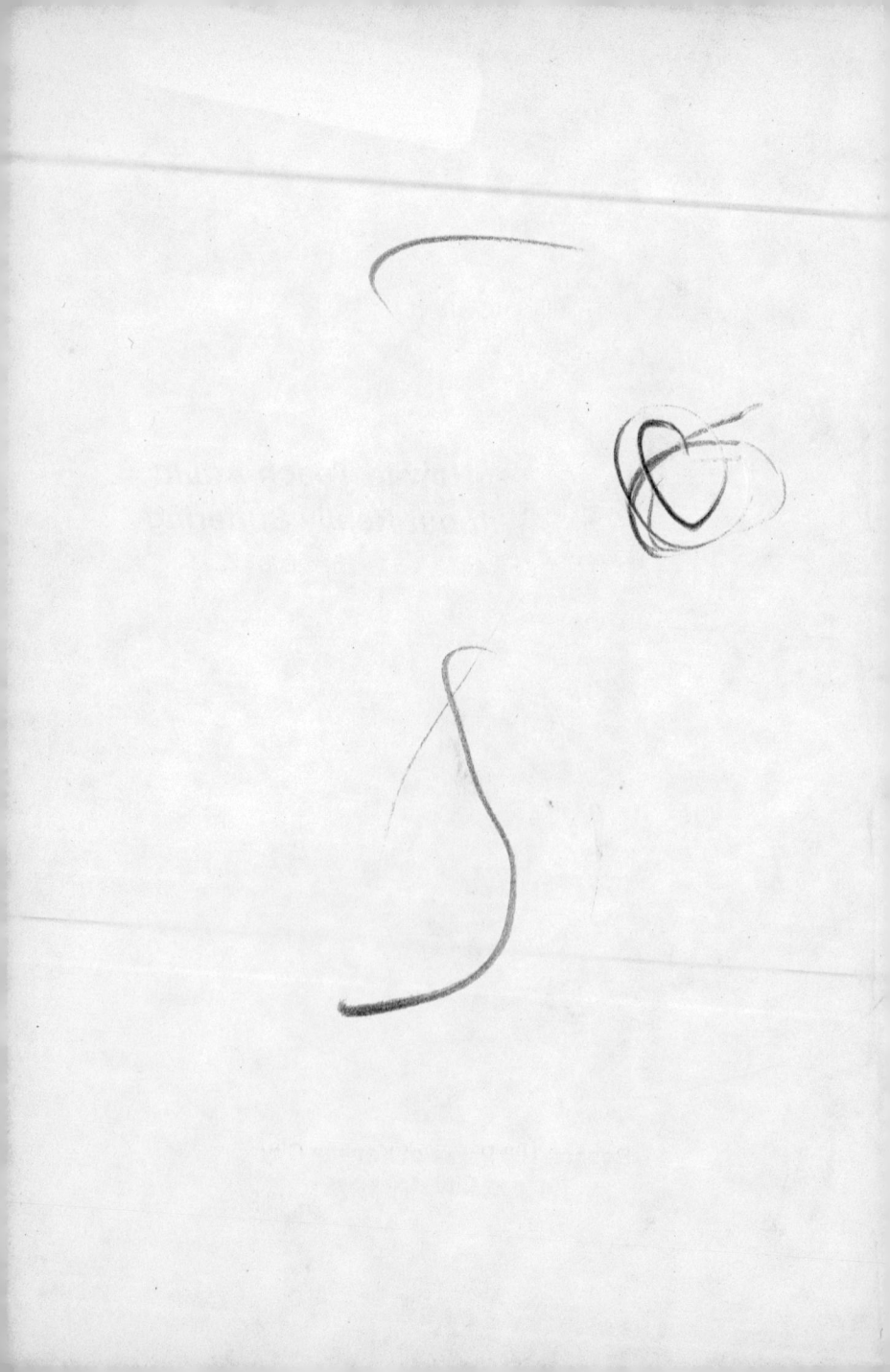

How to Teach Adults
Without Really Suffering

Compiled by
Wesley Tracy

Beacon Hill Press of Kansas City
Kansas City, Missouri

Copyright, 1976
Beacon Hill Press of Kansas City

ISBN: 0-8341-0407-5

Printed in the
United States of America

Permission to quote from the following copyrighted versions of the Bible is acknowledged with appreciation:

The Living Bible (TLB), copyright © 1971, Tyndale House Publishers, Wheaton, Ill.

The *New American Standard Bible* (NASB), copyright © The Lockman Foundation, 1960, 1962, 1963, 1968, 1971.

The *Revised Standard Version of the Bible* (RSV), copyrighted 1946 and 1952.

Contents

Preface	6
Part I—The Adults We Teach	**7**
Chapter 1: If I Could Only Understand You Richard Lee Spindle	8
Chapter 2: U-35 Wesley Tracy	24
Chapter 3: "Singles" Is More than a Tennis Term Neil B. Wiseman	37
Chapter 4: The Forgotten Age-group F. Franklyn Wise	47
Chapter 5: The New Minority Melvin Shrout	58
Part II—Foundations from Which We Teach	**66**
Chapter 6: Stand Here Oscar F. Reed	67
Chapter 7: Toward a Philosophy for Adult Christian Education Donald S. Metz	81
Part III—Practices for Teachers	**89**
Chapter 8: When Jesus Taught the Adult Class Wesley Tracy	90
Chapter 9: Teaching for Transformation Ruth Henck	101
Chapter 10: Grow and Go Earl C. Wolf	108
Chapter 11: Organizing for Nurture and Outreach Tom Barnard	119
Chapter 12: Seen and Noted Waulea Renegar	129
Reference Notes	140

Preface

The Bible boldly tells us *"Through the grace of God we have different gifts. If our gift is . . . teaching let us give all we have to our teaching."** This biblical command precisely expresses the purpose of this book. Hopefully this bit of paper and ink can help Christian teachers of adults to more effectively give all they have to their teaching.

We believe that this book on the basics of Christian adult education will be profitable to the serious teacher. It is not a book of gimmicks. It is not a book of clever methods. Too many teachers today nourish the notion that clever methods in themselves will cure the "common-cold" attitude toward adult education in the church. Methods without the proper foundations in theology, philosophy, and objectives, however, are like roses without roots—cut flowers that quickly fade.

Thus the authors of this book have not dealt extensively with methods. Many books on creative methods are available. So, while not neglecting this aspect, this book seeks to help teachers with such foundational things as Christian beliefs, philosophy of education, Christian psychology, organization, training, goals, and better understanding of the people they teach.

As the editor of this book, I want to thank each contributor. Each one has distinguished himself or herself in the field of Christian education. Each one worked hard on the assignment. I must further thank the members of the editorial committee which guided this project from its inception: Dr. Kenneth Rice, Dr. Donald Metz, Mr. Donald G. Whitlock, Mrs. Ethel Bailey, Rev. Robert Troutman, Rev. Melton Wienecke, and Dr. Earl C. Wolf.

—WESLEY TRACY

*Romans 12:6-7. From *The New Testament in Modern English*, copyright © by J. B. Phillips, 1958.

Part 1
THE ADULTS WE TEACH

Chapter 1

If I Could Only Understand You

*Toward a Psychology of Adult
Christian Education*

Richard Lee Spindle

Many try to dismiss the importance of adult education by resorting to the persistent "old dog" adage. "You can't teach an old dog new tricks!" they insist. Canine lovers will tell you that this claim is a vile lie, perpetrated and repeated by those who are ignorant of dogs. Zeigler insists that "Adults aren't old dogs. Furthermore, you *can* teach a dog what he wants to be taught if the teacher knows more than the dog, and knows how to handle dogs."[1] Educational psychology has taught us that adults can continue to learn indefinitely—regardless of chronological age.

Adult education has existed from the beginning of time. Churches and synagogues have historically been the

---

RICHARD LEE SPINDLE is chairman of the Department of Christian Education at Nazarene Bible College, Colorado Springs, Colo. He earned the A.B., Th.B, and M.A. degrees at Bethany Nazarene College. He did graduate work at Baylor University and holds the Master of Religious Education and Doctor of Education degrees from Southwestern Baptist Theological Seminary. Before joining the faculty of Nazarene Bible College, he served local churches as minister of education, associate pastor, and pastor.

center of education. The Hebrews taught children, youth, and adults in the synagogue. The early Christian Church conducted "catechumenal training" mainly for adults. This was probationary training for church membership. Monastic training (fourth to tenth centuries) was primarily for adults. A great thrust of the sixteenth-century Reformation was Martin Luther's Bible training. Although the modern Sunday school movement began to 1780 to teach "ragged children of England," it has evolved as the great Christian educative agency for "well-dressed adults of America" and the world. World War II gave great impetus to adult education. Adults were forced to learn new skills and research new and uncharted realms of knowledge.

Various indicators seem to point to the fact that we are in the early stages of a great surge in adult education. The phenomenal growth of community colleges in America indicates that adults are responding to a multifaceted and interest-oriented curriculum. The emergence of continuing education programs in business, industry, schools, and the church indicates a belief that adults can continue to learn. Recent statistics of the U.S. Bureau of Census indicate that the world of the immediate future will be a world of adults.

> Never before in history has the interest in education been as intense as it presently is. The significance of this statement is amplified by the fact that "adult education is the largest and fastest growing segment of American education."[2]

We live on the eve of an explosion of adult education in our world.

What should be the response of the church?

How should the church plan to meet the challenge of adult education? A first step should probably be to discover the unique ways in which adults approach a learning situation. How do adults learn? The following are some assumptions and suggestions of which the teacher of adults in the local church should be aware.

Adults Are Experience-laden

Experience is a most valuable commodity in our society. No adult is without experience.

One is not born with experience.

It is not a gift or endowment.

Wealth or prestige cannot provide it.

Education does not necessarily provide it.

It is something available to all adults, and all adults have varying kinds and amounts.

No two adults have the same experience.

Since each experience is unique and distinctive to the "experiencing" person, it then becomes important and of value to all other persons.

Experience is not necessarily measured or valued by bulk, quantity, or chronology. Despite chronological age, experience may be limited to a few areas and a few people and represent a narrow world view.

Experience is not necessarily valued by the impact or dynamic of any particular experience or set of experiences.

Because it is *your* experience and uniquely from your vantage point or frame of reference, then it has value to *me*. The intensity or degree of its value to me is in proportion to the degree or way in which it meets some felt need of mine or relates to my self-concept. Its value is only potential, however, until you share it with me.

A program of adult education in the local church should offer opportunity for such sharing of experience.

Adults Are Goal-oriented

Unlike children and youth, adults do very little without goal or purpose. Children step over cracks in the sidewalk and walk on fences just because it is fun—but for no real reason. Teens play ball and swim and incessantly drive cars just for fun. Adults normally act in the light of some goal.

They play golf and jog and go to the health spa for a purpose—a healthy body. They drive a car with a goal—to go to work, to go to church, to go on vacation, to go to the store. They attend certain educational classes because of what these experiences can do to help them reach some goal—mental development, spiritual growth, skill development, etc.

Adults live in and believe in a goal-oriented society. Life is not lived haphazardly or without attention to certain rules, norms, laws, mores, and goals.

For adults to respond to adult education in the local church, clear and specific and reasonable and need-related and interest-related goals should be set and stated and understood and followed.

Adults find security and meaning in the guidance which goals provide.

Adults Are Problem-centered

Adults reside in a world of problems and problem-solving. Most adult vocations deal with the explanation of, prevention of, and/or solution of problems of some kind. Jerold Apps suggests that "every person has problems . . . in his work, with his spouse, understanding his children."[3]

Adults have independence. Such independence means that one has the ability to recognize and solve certain problems.

Adults have responsibilities. Every normal adult is in authority over somebody or something. Such authority and responsibility demands that they spend much time dealing with, coping with real, concrete, "earth" problems.

Because of this problem-centered orientation, *adults are inclined to seek for and respond positively to education or training which will help them better meet and effectively solve their problems.*

Adults Are Fixation-prone

Edward Thorndike, educational psychologist of the early 1900s, disputed with many notable thinkers by saying that adults are not "set" mentally at age 25. He suggested that adults can go on learning and developing indefinitely; however, it is true that there remains a human tendency—especially for adults—to become fixed, set, or habituated in ways or modes of thinking and doing. Adults are influenced by customs and traditions and commonly accepted ideas and actions. The normal human adult response to change is negative.

Adults indicate their tendency toward fixation when they say such things as: "I never did it that way before!" "I have always done it this way!" "I did not know there was any other way to do it!"

Adults find a sense of security in predictability and sameness. Once a successful way of doing something is found, the adult tends to adopt that way and become fixed in it. Change then may become painful to him.

This proneness to fixation, however, need not become a prison. Adults can break free and learn and adopt new and different ideas and approaches to life.

Adult Christian education can serve to cause a constructive discontent with the status quo and deliver one from the bondage of fixation and sameness in living.

Adults Are Influenced by Group Awareness

The adult, in our society, is quite aware of the group. Our government is a group approach and not an individual or one-man rule. Most of our social institutions—church, school, business, and industry—are group-directed.

The democratic concept touches and influences most all areas of our lives. The adult likes to *be* part of a group. He likes to *feel* part of a group. He is recipient of group pressures and group benefits as well. There is a certain protection and fulfillment in community.

Because of our group-oriented society, adults become somewhat other-directed. They are enabled to move outside themselves and move toward "socialization."

Adults Are Self-conscious

Self-concept influences adult action. Many adults exist with a grossly unrealistic self-appraisal. Some see themselves with a much too low self-image.

During the adult years—if not before—a person should arrive at a somewhat realistic appraisal of self. Adults need to identify various areas of talent, ability, and expertise. Areas of life that need development also must be identified. Men and women need to formulate a personal philosophy of both life and death. One needs to think through to his very self.

Who am I?
What do I really believe?
Where am I now in my "life-trek"?
Where am I going?
How will I arrive where I aim to go?

Adult education helps us to arrive at a better view of ourselves. *The adult Christian education program should help the individual define himself among the local church group and arrive at a satisfactory and realistic self-image.*

Adults Are Culture-clad

Adults have lived long enough and experienced

enough of a culture to begin to live out that culture. Culture-clad customs and ideas and feelings are evident. The longer he lives, the more acculturated the adult becomes.

Men and women become able to identify and live out the proprieties of culture. Such a discovery makes for better social acceptance and adjustment. Despite the reaction of some to the strictures of culture, no normal adult functions meaningfully by rejecting all that is culturally acceptable. All adults are touched by acculturation. No adult is exempt from the influence of cultural propriety.

Awareness of cultural propriety and cultural expectation is a forward step in the process of civilization. Cultural concern is an indication of active involvement in the civilizing process. The attempt to understand and break down various cross-cultural barriers is another step in the civilizing process.

Paul Bergevin, in *A Philosophy for Adult Education,* writes: "The civilizing process is a corporate, social movement involving the whole of society, as it moves from barbarianism toward refinement in behavior, tastes, and thought."[4]

Every attempt one makes to understand culture and intelligently relate cultures is a move toward the development of a healthy and realistic world view.

A healthy local church teaching-learning situation helps adults encounter the various reasons for cultural development and better relate to an ever expanding world view.

Adults Have Individual Expertise

Dr. James Williams writes: "No adult is without authority and influence over someone."[5] A parent exerts influence over children. A teacher influences students. A foreman influences other workers. A group member exerts influence over various other group members. This dynamic of exerting influence may occur in an informal group at a social event or over a cup of coffee in one's home. It may occur at a formal group like a Sunday school class.

There is a certain authoritativeness about adulthood. Adults seem to speak with a certain power or expertise because of their experience. They have developed certain skills—communicative skills, social skills, manual skills—to survive in the world.

Each adult is good at something! Few—if any—adults are totally lacking in a skill or an ability. Most adults move from a stance of "many irons in the fire and none of them hot" to a stance of "fewer but hotter irons." Interest, effort, and skill narrow in on a specific area of affinity and ability. Each adult seems to feel the need to become a kind of expert in a particular area. Each adult seems to want to contribute his unique part to better the outlook of the whole of mankind.

Adult Christian education, rightly done, can make use of those unique areas of individual expertise. It can also help an adult narrow his interests and efforts to certain areas for maximum service.

Adults Are Fun-loving

The normal adult in our culture loves to have fun. Those who cannot or will not have fun seem to gravitate toward hospital rooms and psychiatrist offices.

There is a certain release and relaxation for adults in fun and humor situations. Such emotional outlets are apparently healthy for the total person. They serve as open "pressure valves" through which much pent-up emotional and psychical strain is released. Adult fun times can be therapeutical!

Another benefit is that adults see each other as equals

and very human in occasions of fun and humor. Steve Allen, noted American comedian, suggests: "Humor is a social lubricant that helps us get over some of the bad spots. ... Humor is a humanizing agent."[6]

In an open and informal approach to adult education, one has the opportunity to express and develop his sense of humor and find release and fulfillment in a fun situation. *The Christian adult education situation should be fun!*

Adults Are Service-directed

Through childhood and youth, your adult students were in the process of continually receiving. They received guidance, protection, and training. They were constantly on the receiving end of much of the activity of life.

Most adults reach a point where they are no longer fulfilled or satisfied to be constantly receiving. They want to produce. They want to contribute. They want to give. They want to minister. They want to serve.

The adult, at some point in his development, looks outside the windows of himself and notices that life is slipping by. He looks back at himself and wonders how much he has done for the betterment of mankind. The Christian adult wonders how much he has done for God. Often he senses an urgency to leave the signet of his life on the clay of passing time.

Good adult Christian education provides more than "inside the four walls thought provocation." *The adult religious education plan should provide for adults to serve God and others.*

Adults Are Freedom-focused

The adult has moved from the total dependence of early childhood and the limitations of youth to an adult independence and freedom. The adult naturally resists that which binds, limits, or militates against personal freedom. He will avoid a situation where there are a lot of restrictions. He will shun situations where someone tries to tell him what he needs to know.

Bergevin reminds us that "if we are to realize our potential, the adult learning process must become a creating, releasing experience rather than a dulling series of passively attended indoctrination exercises."[7]

Today's adults respond to situations free of bondage, limitation, restriction, and red tape. *They will attend adult Christian Sunday school classes where there is a relaxed, informal, creating, and releasing atmosphere.*

Adults Need to Be Involved

Adults respond better to situations in which they have been active. They should be involved in planning, implementing, administering, and evaluating the adult Christian education program.

In a sense, this interest in involvement is inclusive of each of the preceding 11 statements. Jerold Apps writes:

> The success of any religious education program depends on involvement, not only involvement of participants in various facets of the program, but involvement of volunteers to lead small and large group discussions, teach the more formal classes, coordinate the more informal and less organized learning experiences, and to plan and administer the entire program.[8]

Through a program of adult Christian education that seeks involvement of each adult, there is the opportunity to:

1. Share the wealth of one's *experience*.
2. Work toward meaningful *goals*.
3. Solve personal *problems*.
4. Free oneself from numerous *fixations*.
5. Define oneself in a *group*.

6. Arrive at a realistic *self*-appraisal.
7. Learn about and live out *cultural* proprieties.
8. Develop *individual expertise* in some realm.
9. Express and develop a sense of humor and find release in an adult *fun* situation.
10. *Serve* real human needs.
11. Express oneself in an informal, creative, and *free* way.
12. Find *involvement* to shape and mold one's total being.

Teaching adults does not mean "telling them what you think they ought to know."

Teaching adults does not mean "sit still and listen to me preach."

To teach adults is to guide and direct and enable them to encounter and respond to truth.

The following dynamics have proven effective in adult Christian educative situations.

Effective Dynamics in Adult Christian Education

Dialogue. The teacher of adults should be able to direct adults in dialogue. Research has shown that personality changes result from meaningful dialogue. If adults are viewed as persons who are to be told and taught and talked down to, their image of themselves is threatened. Many will soon withdraw. Adults have much to learn from one another. They become teachers of one another.

Modern communication has challenged much that we believe is important in human relationships. A loss of community occurs with the breakdown of the primary speaking relationships. Some believe that without "face-to-face relations, the cement of community will crumble and dissolve."[9]

Large-scale efforts are being made to channel our unthinking habits and our purchasing decisions and our thought processes by using insights from psychiatry and the social sciences. Many of these efforts to influence man are below the level of awareness—often subliminal and called "the hidden persuaders." Packard says that "we are manipulated more than we realize."[10]

When adults come from the world of manipulation, they resist being talked down to or in any way manipulated. They deeply desire and need interaction and dialogue.

The "dialogical teacher" believes that the hearer is as important as the speaker.

1. He incorporates dialogue into whatever method he uses.

2. He is alert to the meanings his students bring to the moment of learning.

3. He attempts to help his students formulate their own questions and meanings.

4. He recognizes himself as a resource person who uses his knowledge and skill to bring the student and the gospel together.

5. He is not defensive about the content he presents. He allows for discussion of the pros and cons.

6. He speaks and acts as educator but departs from his teaching plan without undue anxiety. He is not overwhelmed by the pressure to "teach the lesson."[11]

Dialogue means giving the other person time to speak.

Dialogue means getting to know each other as persons.

Dialogue is unafraid of personal encounter.

Dialogue allows for and—at times—invites disagreement with oneself and one's ideas.

Dialogue seeks to give affirmation to others.

The teacher of adults in the local church should develop his abilities to direct dialogue. He should:

1. Enlist and involve class members in active participation.

2. Encourage each to verbalize his thoughts and feelings.

3. Guide class members as they explore uncharted territory.

4. Probe to uncover deeper truth.

5. Verbally recount and reflect what has been said.

6. Reinforce a member's comment.

7. Serve as a resource person and guide class members to appropriate materials and resources to help answer their questions.

Identification. There is a twofold need for identification in adult education. *First,* the adult learner needs to identify with a great cause and with a strong personality. The cause of the gospel and the Church of Jesus Christ offers a profound reason for living and dying. The teacher of adults in the local church should be one who has earned the respect and confidence of the adults. *Second,* the adult learner learns more and responds more positively when his teacher makes the learning experience a cooperative endeavor. The teacher of adults needs to enter the learning experience as a fellow learner and creative listener.

The Christian teacher identifies with his students in their questioning, in their probing, and in their pain. He identifies with them when they socialize, when they laugh and joke, and when they want to talk to him as a person.

He spends much time cultivating a listening ear. This time spent in listening helps build good relationships with people. "As we listen to people, we help them break out of their skin-enclosed isolation and enter into the community of experience and discover their potential."[12]

Many teachers find it difficult to be silent. "For most of us, 10 seconds of silence seems like 10 hours of time."[13]

Our human tendency is to jump in with chatter and keep the "noise ball" rolling. Most of us are so geared to projecting ourselves and our ideas with persuasion that we forget or resist the significance of silence in teaching.

Listening urges us to identify with individual class members. "Listening demands that we enter actively into another person's thinking and try to understand just what is going on within him."[14] The listener skilled in the art of reply becomes a sounding board, an echo chamber, and through the experience of being listened to, the troubled person often discovers himself anew.[15]

Identify with your class members as a person. Let them feel the equality of the ground on which you both stand. Don't yield to the old "master-servant" idea!

Identify with your class members as a fellow learner. Let them feel that you both are involved in a cooperative and continuing quest for truth.

Identify with your class members as a genuinely interested listener. It is one thing to *hear* the sound of their voices as they talk. It is another thing to earnestly *listen* for meaning and significance in what they say. Poor listeners can destroy adult learning situations!

Service. "Teachers of adults in the local church, you are actually involved in a cycle of service!"

You are not an authoritarian!

You are not a dictatorial teller of stories!

You are not a computer programmed with all the answers!

You are—first and foremost—a servant!

You are a guide!

You are a learning leader!

Your task is: to *minister* to *real human needs* by sharing with others in *finding* and *responding* to *truth*.

The so-called one-hour's performance on Sunday

morning is—at most—only one-fourth of your total responsibility. Further, it may *not* even *be* the most important part. A teacher's cycle of service is a servanthood ministry. It involves the following:

1. *Learning About Your Class Members*
Know them as individuals.
Know their talents, abilities, and strong points.
Know their weaknesses, dislikes, and quirks.
Know something about their family backgrounds.
Know—above all—their *needs!*

2. *Pursuing Continual Personal Improvement*
Focus on individual needs when you read the lesson.
Focus on individual needs in Bible reading and prayer.
Prepare and share in the teacher training session.
Use creative approaches in sharing the truth in the classroom.

3. *Leading Your Class in Sharing in Order to Understand and Respond to Truth*
Keep the class session relaxed, informal, open.
Allow freedom of expression to a degree.
Refrain from posing as the authority.
Do not aim to get a concensus.
Focalize on the "kernel of truth" for the day. Don't feel bound and pressured to cover the lesson.
Repeat the kernel of truth several times in various ways.
Give direction in actualizing or living out the truth.
Regularly ask for accountability.
You must lead by example! You model the role!

4. *Serving Them During the Week*
Personal calls in members' homes cannot be measured by human value standards.
Stop by to check on the baby's cold.

Phone to congratulate Johnny for making the scholastic honor roll at school.
Write a note to express appreciation for one's Wednesday night testimony.
Share lunch together during a busy workweek.
Schedule coffee times together.
Schedule recreation outings.
Provide regular, varied fellowship times for the whole class.
Serve them more intently in crisis times: loss, new baby, marriages, illness, important decisions, death.
Promote a servant spirit among your members.
Show that all are workers together with God!

Yours is not meant to be the *linear concept* that views the teacher as making a visit or two per week, performing for an hour on Sunday morning, and then resting on his laurels. Rather, yours is the *cyclical concept* of learning the individual needs of your class members, preparing to meet those needs through continuing personal improvement, leading your class in sharing in order to understand and respond to the truth, and then serving your class during the days of the week. It is in the contacts made between Sundays that you come again face-to-face with individual human needs. Here the beautiful and exciting cycle of service begins to roll again.

As the teacher of adults continually persists in giving himself to this kind of service, human needs are met, personal problems are solved, spiritual growth is fostered, and maturing Christians evolve who, in turn, give themselves in service to others.

Chapter 2

U-35

Toward an Understanding of Today's Young Adults

Wesley Tracy

"U-35—isn't that the magic whitener in that new toothpaste?"

"No, dummy, U-35 is the grime gobbler in that new green detergent."

"Are you ever out of it! U-35 is a rocket—a new secret weapon."

If this were a multiple-choice quiz, the correct answer would be "None of the above." U-35 is simple shorthand for "under 35"—adults under 35 years of age.

In the United States alone there are some 55 million young adults between the ages of 18 and 35. By 1980, that number will swell to 66 million. The sheer force of their

---

WESLEY TRACY is young adult curriculum editor, Department of Church Schools, Church of the Nazarene. He holds degrees from Bethany Nazarene College (A.B.) and the University of Missouri (M.A.). He has done graduate work at Nazarene Theological Seminary, Valparaiso University, and Midwestern Baptist Theological Seminary.

Rev. Tracy served as a pastor for 12 years. He is the author of *New Testament Evangelism Today* and *Sex and the Single Christian* and is the compiler/editor of this book.

numbers makes them a major factor in the present and future of the world. This is the largest young generation that the world has ever known.

It is important that the Church study this generation, for in them we see what Gibson Winter calls "a giant prism that reflects what is happening to society, revealing the best and worst features of the times."[1] Further, in the U-35 generation we see the future. Their causes, values, and lifestyles are harbingers of what is to come.

Is the Generation Gap Real?

The huge number of the U-35s is not the only thing that calls our attention to young adults. They have already become the most influential generation yet. They have been bold in their criticism of society, arrogant in their rejection of authority, and insatiable in their demand for change. They have marched for civil rights, burned buildings and draft cards, defied police, and developed their own moral codes.

They have taken in the dirty laundry of society and waved it in the faces of the older generation. Their shrieks have awakened society to the enormous problems of poverty, racism, war, pollution, overpopulation, unemployment, and depersonalization.

Some mistakes have been made by the young adult generation. Being raised in an "instant-everything" age, they thought that total changes could be made before breakfast and that the state of affairs was totally the fault of their parents' generation alone. One of the weaknesses of the young adult revolution is its lack of historic consciousness. This lack has led to the further misconception that their generation is the first to take life seriously and ask the questions and support the causes they have asked and supported.

Despite the appearance of a cleavage between generations, the gap is more superficial than it might first appear. The U-35s have their roots in history, whether they realize it or not. Their revolution is actually more a *fruition* of cause and effect than a true *revolution*. Look at the history of the twentieth century and you can see that the young adult expressions were predictable. They fit into what one would expect to happen.

Allen J. Moore says, "Many of the causes supported by young adults are actually the same causes championed by adults which now have been taken up by the younger generation.... The young adult culture is really an extension of the larger culture."[2]

With Good Reason

The two generations are united around more causes than they realize. But this is not to deny that real differences do exist. Some of the things that many U-35s have rejected should have been rejected.

Materialism Resisted. The younger generation rebelled against materialism. In all honesty, had not the older "depression generation" lost sight of the fact that it is more important to make a *life* than to make a *living?* The extent of this rebellion is seen in that, in a recent year, more Harvard graduates went into the Peace Corps than into business careers.

Religion Rejected. In general, young adults had good reason to reject the religion of their parents. They saw their parents and their grandparents lose faith in God and in the Bible. As Moore puts it, "The parents of the present young adult generation broke with orthodoxy, embraced religious liberalism, and to a large extent dropped out of churches."[3]

Probably no generation has been treated so shabbily as today's U-35s when it comes to matters of faith. The rug was jerked out from under them. Young adult faith is a jumbled confusion. This results from such theological debacles as "demythologizing the Bible," secularism, "God is dead" theory, and the "man come of age" doctrine. The latter may be the most fatal heresy known in Christian times. It is the notion that the race is finally reaching maturity, so it no longer needs God as a Problem-Solver or Soul-Saver.

Vital Christianity was at a low ebb during the childhood and adolescence of today's young adults. The gospel became social rather than redemptive. The churches they were *sent* to were little more than mental hygiene centers. The sermons they heard were devoid of supernatural redemption and oozed with mere psychologisms.

The church seemed to be engaged in trying to destroy itself by actually promoting such things as premarital sex and secularism. Churchmen hastened to faddishly baptize as Christian anything they saw thriving in the world: civil rights, situation ethics, secularism, and finally atheism itself.

A friend reported to me that he was studying for the ministry at a large denominational seminary in Iowa. He recalled a statement by one of his professors that caused him to drop out. "Of course we know," the teacher said, "that Jesus' death on the Cross is an object lesson in love. But we also know that it is ridiculous to believe that the death of a Jewish prophet 2,000 years ago can in any way atone for our sins. Of course, gentlemen," he continued, addressing the class of young preachers-to-be, "you can't go out into the old, conservative Midwest and say that. But every time you step into the pulpit, you can leave a reasonable doubt."

That is the kind of religious heritage that the young

adult generation has received. Consequently they have become a generation of seekers experimenting with playboyism (neo-hedonism), Ayn Rand's objectivism (religion of selfishness), the Diggers (hippie cult of poverty), the drug cults, Zen Buddhism, transcendental meditation, humanism, and Satanism.

What about young people who have come from homes where the above religious abuses did not exist? Why do so many of them lose their way? There may be a variety of reasons, but a principal one is the fact that for many years now the home has not been the primary influence on youth. The rapid urbanization of society has made school and peer-group influences more powerful than the home.

Scientism Defrocked. One of the most hopeful signs of the seventies is the way the U-35s have defrocked the high priests of scientism. Their parents and grandparents hailed the physicists, chemists, psychiatrists, and the white-gowned researchers as prophet, priest, and king.

Vernon C. Grounds notes that "western civilization has bowed down before the shrine of reason, an exclusive reliance on man's unaided powers of logic and intelligence. . . . [This is] an idolatry which . . . rules out . . . divine revelation . . . poetic institution or philosophical insight or prophetic vision."[4]

Scientism is a dehumanizing tyrant. We regressed so far that thousands of educated people were made to believe (through behavioristic psychology) that whatever was true for a white rat in a small, dark box in a lab was also true of human beings. This debilitating doctrine is only slightly updated today. As Dr. Sigmund Koch of Boston University writes, "The more sophisticated and recent form of the image holds man to be an information-processing entity operating on the principles of a binary digital computer programmed to conform to payoff criteria similar to the rewards of [the hungry rats]."[5]

Dr. Theodore Roszak, history professor at California State College, observes that "the crushing inhumanity of a rationalistic world view has finally been recognized by this generation as the distinctive psychic disease of the age which can and must be remedied."[6] And young adults are searching. In the absence of a true religious heritage, they are trying everything: Eastern religions, American Indian folklore, Yoga, drugs, occultism, and spiritism. It remains for the Church to offer them a dynamic Christianity that will meet their needs. The U-35s are, as Sara Davidson points out, "a generation of seekers, a generation whose world boundaries were shattered by drugs, politics, street-fighting, encounters, communes, or rapid social change, and who came to believe in the possibility of an answer, a key that would make life better immediately."[7] U-35s by their seeking actions have declared themselves friendly toward faith.

With good reason the young adults have rebelled against the materialism, empty religion, and reason-idolatry of their fathers. This is not to justify their methods of rebellion, but simply to say that it should not come as a surprise.

Sexual permissiveness, another area of the revolution, is not good, but was nevertheless predictable. It isn't as though today's young people created liberal sex codes out of thin air. Movies and television have been glamorizing the adulterous life-style for many years. The tolerance for sexual expression found among the young has indeed been evolving in adult society for a long time, as the Kinsey reports testify.

We know that each generation, indeed each individual, is answerable to God for his own actions. But as workers with young adults, we need to know that U-35s came by some of their foibles and failures honestly. They didn't invent them all on their own.

U-35 Developmental Tasks

Three basic developmental tasks confront the young adult: identity, intimacy, and productivity.

Identity or Self-definition. This task of discovering who and what I am bridges adolescence and adulthood. That is, the search for self-definition or identity begins in the teen years and frequently extends into adulthood. It means testing the options open to the individual. Self-definition in today's mixed-up society "involves selecting out of a fragmented collection of expectations, relationship, and ideals those which are most meaningful and putting them together into an integrated definition of life."[8]

Discovering identity means moving past the self-concepts fostered by what others have said one is to the real person inside. The important thing to communicate to young people battling an identity crisis is that they are created in God's image and are objects of divine love.

Self-definition also involves choosing the right cause or vocation to give one's life to. Failing to find a cause or purpose greater than himself will seriously cripple the self-image of the young adult. One of the characteristics of this age-group is the need for great causes. In our teen-oriented society, young adult causes are in short supply. Can Christian education help here?

Intimacy. This is the dominating task during the young adult years. It is "the relationship in which people know one another, support one another, share their lives and identify their interests with one another."[9] This search for significant friendships and meaningful sexual relations will concern the young adult constantly until it is resolved.

If the search for intimacy is unfruitful, crippling isolation and loneliness result.

Repeated failure in the search for intimacy may result in the young adult cutting himself off from other persons. "Walls, barriers and prejudices protect the young adult who fails in his quest for intimacy. What starts out as protective isolation usually leads to an empty loneliness."[10]

Marriage, however, does not automatically solve the intimacy problem. Frequently what Eric Erickson calls *isolation a deux* results. That is, "two people living in the same house, but unwilling and unable to relate openly and intimately with each other. Invisible walls surround each partner, protecting, but at the same time isolating one from the other."[11]

Meaningful intimacy grows out of resolution of the search for identity and out of openness, honesty, and voluntary vulnerability in relationships.

It is easy to see how strategic the intimacy struggle is to the eight human-development tasks listed by Havighurst:[12]

1. Selecting a mate
2. Learning to live with a marriage partner
3. Starting a family
4. Rearing children
5. Managing a home
6. Getting started in an occupation
7. Taking on civic responsibility
8. Finding a congenial social group

Productivity. This task requires the young adult to choose either a life of self-absorption that serves selfish satisfaction, or a productive life that contributes to the well-being of society. The immature regress inwardly and seek only that which profits them personally. Meaningful work is the way most mature persons move toward productivity.

Young adults by the millions have flooded the labor market. The consequent shortage of jobs proves a real handicap to young adults struggling with the developmental task of productivity, especially to the uneducated, the poor, and persons of minority races.

Problems of Young Adults

Sex Problems. It would be almost impossible to overestimate the influence of sexual matters upon young adults. Sex is a dominant force. And the prolonged adolescence required by our society through extended education requirements shoves the young person into serious sex temptations.

Psychologist Harry Stark Sullivan concludes in *The Interpersonal Theory of Psychiatry* that young adulthood is primarily a time of lust. The genital drive and need for sexual expression are never more firmly felt than during the young adult years. Sex becomes a dominant concern as the young person focuses in on sexual behavior and how to fit it into the rest of life. Christian young people are not exempt from the pressures of sexually related problems.

Another dimension of the sexual problem for young adults is homosexuality, which Dr. James Dobson describes as a contagious disease that is spreading in epidemic proportions. Moore says that this is "generally a problem most characteristic of young adults."[13]

Anomie. This is a term given to the problems related to the disorganization of urbanized man. Various terms are used to describe it, including planlessness, lawlessness, rulelessness, and rootlessness.

This element is urgently present in the U-35 generation. One gauge by which sociologists measure this is the suicide rate. Suicide has been increasing among young adults at an alarming rate. About 1,000 college students kill themselves each year. Some 9,000 more attempt suicide, and nearly 100,000 more threaten to take their own lives.

Related to *anomie* is the dropout problem. Moore's research shows that 60 percent of every freshman class leave college, or are dropped, because they cannot meet school demands. In addition the rootlessness of many noncollege young adults causes them to "drop out" of life and exist in a semicatatonic state.

A real danger exists in the *rulelessness* or *lawlessness* dimension of *anomie*. Young adults, adrift in troubled times, seem to be dangerously near to adopting an extremely selfish individualism which is so close to anarchy that it is frightening.

Crime. Persons under 30 dominate prison populations. The young adult arrest rate for major crimes such as murder, rape, and armed robbery is higher than for any other age-group.[14]

Divorce. This is a young adult problem, but it is also a problem for the Church. If we Christians are going to minister effectively to young adults, we must make up our minds fast about how divorce relates to salvation and participation in church life. Approximately one-half of all divorces involve men and women under 29 years of age.

Mental Health. In our society the traditional landmarks are disappearing like sand castles in the rising tide of new things. This puts great stress upon the mental health of the U-35s searching for identity, intimacy, and productivity. Various forms of psychological depression are prominent in young adults. In addition, 75 percent of the men and women in the United States who suffer from schizophrenia are young adults.

Some Implications for the Church

The concerns treated here have too many implications (even mandates) for the Church for us to deal with them adequately in this brief study. Let us mention only three.

1. *Focus on Learning*

John Doe walks into a certain church for the first time. There's no problem at all about which of the four adult classes to put him in; after all, he is 27 years old and married. So he goes into the "Couples for Christ" class. John may be a college graduate, or a theology professor, or he may have been converted last night in a skid row mission.

He may be interested in studying soul winning or basic Christian doctrines, but that makes no difference—he is shoved right into "Couples for Christ," where the teacher is plowing through Leviticus. His background, aptitudes, and personal preference make no difference, because in this church (as in so many others) no one cares whether he learns anything or not. The Sunday school is focused on mere attendance, not learning. A student cannot reach a point where he can say, "Now I've reached a certain goal. I've finished eight basic courses; now I can go on to something bigger and better." No, the classes just go on and on indiscriminately. His job is to show up, not learn.

The U-35s are interested in learning. Half of them have graduated from or attended college. If they do not find challenging learning opportunities in your Sunday school, they won't be back. For us to fail to teach this generation, adrift without anchors, is a tragedy too painful to contemplate.

The task for curriculum developers, Christian educators, and Sunday school teachers is clear. They must provide an intersection of young adult problems and developmental concerns with Bible truth.

2. *Focus on Koinonia*

The Early Church borrowed the term *koinonia* ("fellowship") from Greek military parlance. The commander of a Grecian traveling troop would at day's end select a camping area. He would designate one spot within the area as the *koinonia*. Every soldier would then put down whatever he was carrying (weapons, food supplies, etc.) in the *koinonia* and then go to find rest and sleep. In the morning, he would receive his assignment for the day. Then he would go to the *koinonia,* and there, from the resources of all the group, he would take whatever he needed to get him through his assignment for the day.

The early Christians related that to their experiences of meeting together in house churches. There they would, from the spiritual resources, fellowship, and support of the whole group, find strength to face the assignment for the day.

Young adults, in their struggles with identity, intimacy, and productivity, must find in our Sunday school classes and our small groups this same supportive fellowship. It may be the best gift we can give.

3. *Focus on Flexibility*

Each of us is apt to think that the way he was saved and the way he is sustained in the Christian life is best for everyone. We must learn that God is bigger than our experience of Him. If we can learn this, we will not make the mistake of trying to turn out all converts with our own personal theological cookie cutter. We must not try to force everyone into our particular pattern. We must be flexible and adaptable enough to meet young adults where they are and let God work through our patience, understanding, and positive regard.

Inflexibility can make us duplicate in our Sunday schools what happened to the duck in the animal school. It seems that the duck was a problem pupil. His teacher observed that, although he was proficient in swimming, he was very deficient in running. Running held a high priority in the curriculum, so the duck was enrolled in a program of remedial running and then reevaluated. The records revealed that not only had the duck failed to improve in running, but he now had sore feet and couldn't swim either.

This parable of the sore-footed duck can be a starting point for examining the flexibility with which we treat young adult individual differences, of which they have plenty and to spare.

Chapter 3

"Singles" Is More than a Tennis Term

Ministering to Today's Single Young Adults

Neil B. Wiseman

"Not more than 10 . . . maybe less than 5." That is the reply a nationally known Christian education specialist recently gave when asked how many evangelical churches (excluding college centers) he knew about which maintained a vital Bible teaching program geared especially to single young adults.

His statement may seem exaggerated, but it illustrates a tough truth. We capture the attention and loyalty of the teen-ager, but practically ignore him in his post-high-school days and early twenties. By implication the church seems to say, "We expect you to drop out during or shortly after high school. Hope you will be back in your twenties or early thirties. Maybe you can return after you

---

NEIL B. WISEMAN serves as chairman of the Department of Religion and college chaplain at Trevecca Nazarene College, Nashville, Tenn. Mr. Wiseman holds degrees from Olivet Nazarene College (Th.B.), Nazarene Theoligical Seminary (M.Div), and Vanderbilt University (D.Min.).

Dr. Wiseman served as a youth pastor and Christian education director before a 14-year tenure in the pastoral ministry. He is author of *The Department Supervisor* and *To the City with Love*. He is a regular contributor of articles to various religious journals.

marry; this Sunday school always offers a fine class for the newly married. You might even like to teach a class after you come back."

Next to the teen years the most serious attrition rate is among young adults between 18 to 30 years of age—a disaster for the church when you consider the loss of vitality for Christian service, new ideas, and future leadership.

Introducing the Single Young Adult

Since most of our churches do not have many single young adults, it is easy to overlook them. Characteristics of the single young adult are not easily defined. But for the teachers of adults there must be the awareness that the single young adult is different in attitude, action, and ability from the teen-ager. At the same time he does not have the same life concerns as the young married, middle, or older adult.

There is infinite variety in the characteristics of unmarried persons in the 18-30-year-old bracket. And while such designations as having reached legal age, finishing formal schooling, achieving full self-support, assuming adult responsibilities, living permanently away from his parental home, completion of military service, and having had a certain number of birthdays may provide useful clues to one's maturity, they do not furnish universally acceptable criteria for deciding who is a young adult. A self-sufficient 17-year-old high school dropout who is economically self-supporting may be considered a single young adult, while his 19-year-old college sophomore brother may be considered a teen-ager.

When we think of young singles we usually mean employed, unmarried persons who live away from their childhood homes. But even this designation has many variables. Some young adults are *students in colleges away from home* who have a continuing interest in the church and at holiday periods are eager to be involved in church life. Then there is the *college student who lives at home;* his blossoming intellectual gifts coupled with his growing need for independence create a special need for ministry.

Many singles are in *military service,* which has a wide influence on social contacts, job opportunities, and the willingness of the young persons to make long-term investments in their futures. Simply because they are usually the larger numbers, *those who have completed their education and have joined the work force* need the most attention in the church's ministry to this age-group. Then, too, *divorced and separated young adults* need a caring ministry. These people often face problems of shattered self-worth, financial pressures, loneliness, and rejection by some church members because of their broken marriage.

In *The Church and Its Young Adults,* J. Gordon Chamberlin provides a useful insight. He says, "Young adults have only one characteristic in common—they are young at the business of being adults."[1]

The young adult years usually include a significant change in former family relationships and efforts to make an independent life. Since the single young adult is inexperienced with independence and because severing the "apron strings" is seldom easy, he or she may experience great stress. Thus he needs the supportive, caring ministry of a spiritually alive Christian young adult group. Such a group can make a lifelong contribution to his spiritual development.

The needs of this age-group are unique and worthy of adequate personnel, budget, planning, and facilities in the local church.

The Pressing Need for Single Young Adult Ministries

Young single adults provide a very productive nearby

field for evangelism in nearly every center of population. But why should a church give high priority to a ministry for single young adults?

• *Young single adults are a significant segment of the general population.* Almost one-third of the people in North America live in central cities, and 75 percent of the total population live in urban areas. Many young adults, especially the college and university trained, view the city as a necessary beginning place to become established in their vocations. One national news magazine estimates the young adult population will gain by 18.1 million during this decade. By the end of this decade, one-third of the U.S. population will be in their twenties and thirties; and many of them will be unmarried and living near your church. So the centers of population are especially in need of a single young adult ministry, but we dare not neglect this ministry even in small towns and rural areas.

• *The Single Young Adult Needs Christ.* Disillusioned by affluence, mobile, often well trained, and sometimes misunderstood by the older generation, these young people need the Saviour. This is the age of the most significant questions of human existence. He is asking: Who am I? Where am I going? What kind of person should I be? What do other people think about me? While during the teen years the young adult *thought* about his or her choice of occupation, mate, and development of personal potential, now the choices clamor to be made. Their quest is for meaning. The church can guide them to the meaning they seek. We must not shrug off this opportunity and responsibility.

• *Few Churches Have a Single Young Adult Ministry.* There may be good reasons for this apparent neglect, but the fact remains that most churches do not reject the single young adult. They simply ignore him. And, like most persons whose spiritual needs are overlooked, the young single becomes less and less interested. His loyalty, involvement, and spiritual life decline. But such a spiritual vacuum may provide a greater possible degree of success to those churches who try to minister effectively to this group.

Elmer Towns offers useful guidance: "Because of their drive for fellowship, arising from loneliness and identity-crisis, young single adults go where there is warmth and opportunities to meet other adults in meaningful settings. They do not want to be treated as special cases, rather as human beings."[2] So the need for such a ministry presses itself upon the caring church when we consider the total lack of such an effort in so many places.

• *The Church Needs the Young Single Adult.* Surely every church everywhere needs a new source of spiritually aggressive people. When fully challenged by the living Lord, the young single adult provides the church with a reservoir of people with new ideas, deepening commitments, enterprising vitality, potential leadership, and new stewardship resources. Here is a target for evangelism with high energy levels that can be channeled into useful service for the Kingdom. Singles are often willing to invest large amounts of time in Christian service. Further, recent studies show that young singles give money at nearly twice the per capita level of other church members.

How Is a Single Young Adult Ministry Built?

Bernard Asbell wrote of John Gardner, former secretary of health, education, and welfare, "Everything he does is focused. He'll say, 'What are the most important issues? What's the one thing we've got to be doing?' He keeps looking for . . . the most important thing we've got to do in the next six months or so. . . . He connects ideas, people, and resources so that something happens."[3] And that is exactly the foundation on which a vital local church ministry for single young adults must be built—ideas, people, and resources must be connected.

Bible Learning That Intersects with Young Adult Concerns. In far too many classes, the lesson consists of unquestioned opinions, childhood prejudices, and outright biblical error. This can change when Bible facts and an application of the Bible to life are taught side by side in the same lesson.

Bible history, background, and geography must be shared. But real life and the Bible must have a head-on collision in your single young adult group. Bible truth and young adult concerns must be brought together. Your class members must be motivated to a loving obedience to God by this question, "What does the Bible say to my present situation?" Single young adults thrive on solid Bible teaching. Thus when the Bible is helpfully applied to life, it becomes one of the very best attractions for increasing the size of your group. Vital Bible learning will deeply challenge attitudes and actions of your group members. Christian growth for believers will result from such challenging teaching, and unbelievers will experience a strange magnetism to groups where this happens.

But how does the average Sunday school teacher accomplish such a demanding goal? Are there practical ways to make the Bible and real life meet in your young singles class? How do we apply the Bible to human affairs?

One experienced Bible teacher makes the application by relating three simple questions to the Scriptures during both his preparation and presentation. These questions are: What does the scripture say? What does it mean? And how can I apply this passage to my life?

Another method is to apply three time frames—*then, always,* and *now.* In the use of *then,* the teacher seeks to share what the original writer of the biblical passage was actually saying to his readers in his time. *Always* is that expositional dimension of the scripture which makes room for the Bible to speak usefully to people in every age, culture, and situation. And the *now* question is answered by applying the passage to the contemporary experiences of the learner in your class.

Group Life. "Community" at the first sounds like a wide spot in the road or a village too small to be called a town. There are some likenesses. My meaning is closer to the old-fashioned idea of fellowship and spiritual togetherness. It is much more than fun and games; a lot more than a battered Ping-Pong table or an overused dart board. It is more than a gripe-gossip session of those who wistfully long for a day when the church will be perfect in every detail.

In a truly meaningful kind of fellowship, the young single adult finds a group of caring spiritual pilgrims who are willing to share their discoveries and sometimes admit their difficulties. Like Wesley's class meetings, time is available for prayers, testimony, and, if needed, confession. This kind of togetherness is usually built by a group who enjoy being with one another as they study the Bible or do some meaningful work for the Saviour or His hurting people. Sports programs and social events are needed on a frequent basis in the single young adult group, but the group should always seek to make those gatherings contribute to the community or fellowship aims of group life.

Leadership. A unique kind of leader is required for single young adults. He or she must be open and have the highest possible motivation to be of service to the group. Since self-discovery kinds of learning are most effective in working with single young adults, the leader must be flexible enough to try new approaches in teaching and see himself as a guide, moderator, or enabler.

The leader must be one who deeply loves young people, one who works diligently at understanding the contemporary young single adult to whom he seeks to minister. He must be a blend of acceptance, openness, love, and steadfast integrity. The leader of young singles must accept the jolts of their penetrating honesty. And it will help if his Christian life is so consistent that others may model his attitudes, dedication, and values in their own lives. The leader's oral teaching should be effective, but it is vastly multiplied when it is consistent with a worthy Christian example lived before those he seeks to lead.

The gentle art of affirmation needs to be a part of the teaching style of the leaders of single young adults. Affirmation is different from flattery. Flattery may be a lie, a half-truth, or a full truth told to manipulate another. But affirmation is that honest, positive truth about another which we are willing to share simply because he needs to hear it. Affirmation is an expression of appreciation for what the person is or a recognition of qualities that God has already built into his life.

To affirm another person does not mean that we fail to recognize his sin if it be present. Some do need to have their sins renounced on occasion. Sin is real; the Cross speaks of its seriousness. Jesus identified sin, but at the same time He appealed to something basic and fine when He called people to be His followers. He quickly recognized the strengths of Zacchaeus, Nicodemus, and the rich young ruler. He did not deny their sin, but He was accepting of them and eager to affirm them as persons of great worth. Jesus loved people. He often found himself meaningfully related to "unlikely" groups such as Pharisees, Samaritans, and fishermen. He called them to be something beyond anything they had ever dreamed possible. He seemed to be charmed and challenged by what people could become. That is the business of the leader of single young adults—the development of potential and possibility in the members of his group.

Young singles want to be taken seriously by their leader. Questions, unusual viewpoints, and half-formed conclusions will be discussed. The dialog provides opportunities to keep Bible absolutes before them. The patient, open leader will have the privilege at the right moment to share Christ as the Solution to the deepest human needs.

The needed leadership qualities of this guide are very demanding—too demanding without divine enablement. But the Lord of the Church can make this kind of leader out of a spiritually sensitive person who eagerly wants to be of help to present-day single young adults.

Self-piloted Programming. For most ministries in the local church it is necessary to provide complete programs, recruit leaders, raise funds, and promote the activities. Not so with single young adults. They want to be involved in the planning, working through the specific details, and sometimes they want to help choose leaders. They should be encouraged to take such responsible leadership. The young single adult has the time, energy, and initiative to effectively accomplish many ministries in the local church. And often he has a better education and greater imagination than his elders. All of these talents should be usefully harnessed for significant spiritual achievement.

It is unnecessary and may be counterproductive for the church to make all the arrangements and set up the agenda for the young singles. They should be instructed to allow their plans to be approved by the proper authorities in the local church and then be encouraged to dream big and accomplish much.

Challenge with Action. Too much of the Christian religion has turned into mere talk. In the stimulating discussion sessions, the young singles will ask, "Why doesn't the church do something to meet the needs of our world?" Answer with your own question, "Why don't you do it?"

Children from broken homes need a big brother or sister. Ghettos need a shade-tree vacation Bible school. The hungry need to be fed. The old need a word of encouragement and someone to help them with practical problems. The educationally disadvantaged need tutors. The church needs overseas missionaries. Home mission churches need a helping hand with remodeling an old church or conducting a community-wide visitation program. Urban ministries in many places need a lay volunteer single young adult who would give one or two years of his life to make a city church come alive again. When these capable, thoughtful young singles ask their questions, "Why doesn't somebody . . . ?" have your own question ready, "How about you?"

Serve up your gospel challenges with a call to disappointments, tears, love, and real victory. Those new adults will respond. Your Sunday school class will become more vital. The class will grow. Who knows what will happen? Under the same Leader, Jesus Christ the Lord, 11 men changed the world nearly 1,950 years ago, and it has never been the same.

Chapter 4

The Forgotten Age-group

The Nature and Needs of Middle Adults

F. Franklyn Wise

Specialists are hired for our children's work; church staffs are crammed with youth experts; young adults are whim-catered to death; senior citizen's clubs are growing like daffodils in April—but whatever happened to our middle adults?

We seem to be giving our adults between the ages of 35 and 55 the same kind of attention that Dr. Samuel Young says he gives the devil—"mortifying neglect."

If the teacher of middle adults is to be of maximum help to his students, he should understand them. During the years between 35 and 55, significant changes occur in all aspects of their lives. For the purposes of this chapter we shall consider individuals who are 35 to 45 years old as

---

F. FRANKLYN WISE is chairman of the Department of Religious Education at Olivet Nazarene College. He has spent some 20 years in college teaching, serving at Trevecca Nazarene College, Malone College, and Olivet Nazarene College.

Dr. Wise received the A.B. degree from Eastern Nazarene College. His M.Ed. and Ph.D. degrees in religious education were earned at the University of Pittsburgh. He has contributed to numerous religious publications. Dr. Wise also served as a pastor for 13 years.

younger middle-aged adults; those who are 45 to 55 we consider older middle-aged adults.

L. J. Bischof observes that "adulthood is a horrendous stage of existence, more to be pitied and prayed about than to be lived through."[1] Middle age in itself, nevertheless, is not as dreadful as many persons describe it. Much of this pessimism currently being expressed is because youthfulness is so highly valued in our society. In reality, middle age has many assets which youth does not have. Individuals who are 55 are more likely to be earning more money than before. Many of them have reached a high level of success and achievement. Most positions of power and prestige in business, politics, and the church are filled by older middle-agers. When individuals get to middle age, they experience greater independence and freedom than they had as young persons. Most, if not all, of their children have left home to establish independent lives. Older middle-aged adults have gained relative financial independence.

What Are Middle Adults Like?

In the last few years psychologists have become especially interested in studying middle-aged adults. Havighurst devised a list of the developmental tasks of adults. He defines a developmental task as "a task which arises at or about a certain period in the life of the individual, successful achievement of which leads to his happiness and to success with later tasks, while failure leads to unhappiness and difficulty with later tasks."[2] The tasks he names are:

> maintaining oneself as an effective worker, which may involve additional schooling or retraining; continuing to relate oneself to one's spouse; assisting teen-age children in becoming responsible adults; relating to aging parents and parents-in-law; establishing and maintaining an economic standard of living congruent with needs; achieving adult civic and social responsibility; main-

taining friendships and social ties; and sustaining leisure-time activities.[3]

Load Shedding

Several dominant trends in the adult years are especially important in middle age. One of these is the process of disengagement or "load shedding."[4]

"Late life for most people is characterized by a reduction in physical activities and social interaction."[5] Beginning in the middle years of middle age, persons shed many responsibilities they formerly carried. For example, when the children no longer need to be driven to school, the mother will disengage herself from the car pool. When children no longer attend public school, the parents have little interest in the P.T.A. As teen-agers outgrow the church youth group, their parents see less reason to be involved in adult activities provided for parents of teen-agers. As individuals age, disengagement increases.

Role Changes

Another dominant trend of middle age is the necessity to make role changes. This characteristic is rooted in the interpersonal relationships, especially those of the family situation, that are altered with age. In the early years of middle age, parents will usually have some teen-age children in the home. By the end of middle age, most, if not all, of the children will be leading an independent life. Middle-aged parents will have to develop relationships with the spouses of their children as well as their children's in-laws.

For some middle-aged adults, grandparenthood involves a joyful role change; for others, a dreaded one. Those who dread assuming the role of grandparent do so because it forces them to acknowledge the reality of the aging process. Individuals who have a strong need to appear young especially resent the role of grandparent.

However, many middle-aged adults like to become grandparents. Grandchildren provide the joyfulness of having children, without the intense investment of energy required of parents. In other words, grandparents can spoil their grandchildren and then send them home to their parents.

As children grow older, middle-aged parents are faced with the necessity of treating their grown adult children as adults, not children. They need to adjust their parent-child relationships to regarding their adult children as dear friends, no longer emotionally dependent youngsters. Middle-aged parents must limit their role as counselors and guides to only those times when they are sought out by their children. If they maintain the hovering concern and "bossing" they did in childhood, they will alienate their children. Consequently, they risk losing the emotional support their children could give them at a time when parents need it very much.

Role change involves developing new relationships with one's own aging parents. In early middle age, one's parents are self-sufficient, active, and healthy. By the end of middle age, many of them are old, sick, and unable to care for themselves. Thus the aged parents require more care; they become more dependent upon their children. Middle-aged adults are often faced with the task of providing care for their parents. In many cases this responsibility involves the decision as to whether the aged parents will be cared for in the home or put in an institution.

Both choices involve undesirable consequences. Aged parents in the home often disrupt family routine and limit the freedom of the family to go away. If the parents become bedfast, they require a heavy investment of time and energy caring for them.

On the other hand, if aged parents are institutionalized, they impose a heavy financial burden. If they did not want to go to the rest home, they are more likely to die sooner than they would have if they had wanted to go. Many elderly persons interpret their being put in an institution as a sign of rejection by their children rather than an expression of love and concern.

Some middle-aged adults must face a role change as a result of the loss of a spouse by death or divorce. Both suicides and divorces begin to increase at age 45. Suicides are common during this period. Whether by natural death, divorce, or suicide, the loss of a spouse during middle age involves drastic and abrupt role changes. Women are faced with the reality that their chances of remarriage lessen with each passing year. Men must learn to cope with loneliness.

Accepting Reality

The third dominant trend of middle age is the necessity of accepting reality. Gradually the individual must face reality, accept it rather than evade it by wishful thinking. Adolescence and early adulthood build their dreams; middle age must look honestly at reality. Have the hopes and aspirations been achieved? What chance is there that they will ever be realized?

Reality acceptance is especially important in four areas: physiological changes, childbearing practices, vocational direction, and death.

First, middle age involves significant physiological changes, especially in women. Around age 40, most women begin their change of life process, menopause. During the next five years, the ovaries gradually cease to produce ova capable of being fertilized. At the end of this process, women no longer can bear children.

Not only do the ovaries cease producing ova, they produce less and less female hormones, estrogen and progestin. The loss of these hormones upsets the delicate balance of the body's glandular balance. As a result, women may experience hot flashes, sweating, headaches, irritability, fatigue, and tingling over their entire body. Fortunately these reactions may be lessened if the body supply is supplemented therapeutically with these hormones.

Other long-range effects may include a lessening of feminine appearance as facial hair becomes coarser, the voice deepens, and the curves of the body flatten out. Some women gain weight. Many experience an increase in joint pain, especially in the fingers. Some women may experience increasing nervousness, apprehension, lack of concentration, uncertainty in the face of unexpected situations, irritability, depressions, and melancholia. Many of these symptoms may be traced to folklore.

The psychological effect of menopause is directly related to the woman's personal attitude. Some women anticipate eagerly the freedom change of life brings. Others who regarded childbearing as especially important to their sense of wholeness dread it. In all cases married women need the comfort and reassurance of their husbands during this period. Women need to feel loved for themselves, not for their ability to have children. The majority of women who are sound in health and mind and well adjusted to their surroundings will pass through the menopause with a minimum of distress.

Men also face physical changes in middle life, although they are not as significant for them as the menopause is for women. The spontaneous occurrence of a male climacteric is still controversial. Many of the symptoms ascribed to this syndrome are common psychoneurotic syndromes in middle-aged and elderly men.

The impact of this change in middle life for men depends to a large extent upon the individual's self-concept. Men who equate masculinity with sexual performance and attractiveness to the opposite sex may dread middle life.

Some of them may engage in "proving behavior" by having illicit affairs. For this reason, middle age for some men is accurately described as a "dangerous age."

Most men will experience little or no trauma with the onset of middle age. They have achieved their sense of worth by investing their energies in their business, vocation, or profession and rearing of a family.

Both sexes must accept the reality of the aging process: The skin becomes coarser and more wrinkled, the hairline recedes and begins to gray, the eyes lose their brightness, and teeth are replaced with dentures. While many cosmetic aids, hair dyes, and contact lenses may soften the physical changes of aging, they do not halt it. They may even make the alterations of age more pronounced and harder to accept.

Middle age increases the danger of disease. The body loses some of its strength; the accumulative effects of stress increase. Heart attacks and high blood pressure become the toll adults pay for their competitive, stress-filled life-style.

The *second* area of reality acceptance in middle age is the effects of child-rearing practices. During childhood, parents could control their children and hope they would turn out well. Adolescents are the visible result of their parents' efforts to a certain extent.

Parents of children who turn out well have few worries. Parents whose children disappoint them face many stresses. They often ask themselves and others, "What did we do wrong?" They experience deep, self-incriminating feelings of failure. Such feelings are especially painful in Christian circles. Parents whose children disappoint them must guard against allowing feelings of bitterness to arise against other parents in the church whose children turned out so well.

While child-rearing practices are very important, they

do not altogether relieve adolescents from bearing the responsibility for their own choices. They may blame their parents, but to a very large degree, adolescents who disappoint their parents had many opportunities to take a different path—opportunities they spurned.

The *third* major area of reality acceptance faced at about age 55 has to do with one's employment. Because of the hiring practices and the current employment picture, adults at this age must face the reality of their vocational direction. Those who have succeeded and who are happy with their jobs will face few problems. Those who feel they have not fulfilled their aspirations and who are unhappy in their jobs will begin to feel "locked in" or "trapped." They must face the reality they cannot at this age change jobs easily. They must accept the fact younger men will be chosen ahead of them for the more prestigious jobs. Individuals who are unhappy in their work tend to generalize their feelings to all other aspects of their lives.

The *fourth* area in which middle-aged adults must face reality is the matter of death. During the previous life stages, young persons could evade the face of death. When young persons attended a funeral, it was usually for an older person. In middle age, the funerals individuals attend are often for friends the same age or just a little older. Gradually middle-agers begin to seriously consider the years left to them. As those years become fewer, the reality of death begins to emerge.

Needs of Middle Adults

What are the needs of middle-aged adults which arise out of these facts? Foremost is the need for emotional support based on genuine understanding. Middle-aged women who face the "empty-nest syndrome" need to have emotional support as they find ways to fill up their time and explore channels into which to divert their love. Women often feel unneeded and unwanted now, especially if they focused their whole life on their "mothering" activities.

Parents who suffer from feelings of parental failure need some intimate fellowship to supplement their spiritual resources. They need persons who care about them but who do not pry into the family affairs. They need to feel they are needed and wanted in spite of what happened to their children. How often these parents want to be with someone who really understands their hidden heartaches.

Middle-agers who are asking, "Where do I go now?" need to have group support which will restore their sense of worthwhileness and purpose. Those left alone, those who chose to be alone, those trapped, those who failed to fulfill their aspirations all need this genuine, loving help.

So often middle-agers are tempted to feel they are tolerated because of their financial or leadership support alone. Especially those who come to the end of middle age and see the younger persons taking over the church leadership roles are tempted to feel lonely and unneeded. Middle-agers have a real need for a strong, supportive group.

Ministry to Middle-aged Adults

The Church must plan its ministry to these adults on the basis of their needs and characteristics. Such a program will give a major segment of time and attention to serving these people and to helping them serve.

The Church must find ways to *use the reservoir of skills and experience this age-group represents.* They have lived a major part of their lives and have experienced many of the trials, temptations, and afflictions which youth and young adults are now facing. They are old enough to identify with the old-age group. Middle-aged adults can and should fill many teaching jobs and leadership roles in every phase of the Church's task.

Does the age gap make it difficult for middle-aged persons to teach adolescents and young adults? One report indicates the ability to understand and communicate with youth is a more important requirement than age for teachers.[6]

As middle-aged adults can find ways to invest their skills in God's kingdom, they will recover a sense of mission and worthwhileness so essential at this period of their lives.

A second avenue of ministry to middle-aged adults is through *the organization of small, intimate social groups.* The usual Sunday school class is a ready-made group of this sort. Such groups may function as Bible study and prayer cells, as well as socializing groups. Middle-aged adults can find in a group of their peers the emotional and spiritual support they need so desperately. Such a group needs to develop trust and openness so the members can feel comfortable sharing the deep hurts and distressing anxieties. In such a group the resources of prayer and God's promises can be brought to bear on their problems and needs.

Obviously such a group must be built on mutual trust and concern. It need not, nor should it be, an exercise in sensitivity training, encounter activities, nor confrontation tactics. Rather the Christian ideal is for the group to be a fellowship, a band of individuals who openly acknowledge their hurts and anxieties to each other and who seek to be ministers of divine enablement one to the other.

Another ministry to middle-aged adults is *through stimulating and creative Bible study.* Too often the adult Bible class serves intellectual pablum instead of steak. Sunday school teachers must recognize the average educational level of middle-agers has risen steadily over the past quarter century. It has been pointed out that "in 1910 only 13.5 percent of those over twenty-five had completed at least four years of high school; by 1973 this figure had risen to 60 percent. In this same period, the percentage of those with four or more years of college rose from 2.7 to 12.6."[7]

Middle-aged adults need to tackle the tough issues in the Bible. They need to bring the issues in their lives under the judgment of God's authoritative Word. Sunday school classes which do not do this fail in their ministry to middle-agers.

The Church should sponsor weekend retreats for middle-aged adults. They need the time for spiritual refueling as much as any age-group in the Church. Since they face heavy responsibilities, vocationally and financially, they need the quiet time to renew their inner selves.

The Last Word

Middle age is a period of life in which society expects individuals to be mature. Maturity is less a chronological concept and more of an emotional, social one. Maturity is defined as being able to handle the changes and the responsibilities of one's age level. It is a time of real role changes and facing of responsibilities. With middle age comes freedom, prestige, and independence; but accompanying these assets are many threats, disappointments, and losses. The Church finds in this age-group its financial and leadership foundation. Middle adults look to the Church for spiritual, intellectual, and fellowship ministry. Through such ministries the Church can enrich the lives of middle adults and in turn the Church herself will be enriched.

Chapter 5

The New Minority

The Nature and Needs of Older Adults

Melvin Shrout

This year 10 percent of the birthday cakes will sport 65 or more candles. Since 1900, the older adult population has quadrupled. Early next century one out of every five persons pounding our pavements will be senior citizens.

In times past, most men dreamed of retirement, but fewer than 5 our of 100 realized it. The current prospect is that 1 person in every 5 now in their thirties will reach this "third age."

Older people are not a new phenomenon, but their large number is an unusual development of our times. They have been dubiously dubbed "the Geritol generation," "the thrown-away generation," "the golden-agers" and "the new minority," and every day this group increases by 1,000 persons.

The "new minority" population bulge has created (or at least made popular) a new science—gerontology, the

---

MELVIN SHROUT is the director of senior adult ministries for the Department of Church Schools, Church of the Nazarene International Headquarters, Kansas City, Mo. Rev. Shrout is an ordained minister and served a 30-year tenure as pastor before accepting his current denominational assignment. He received his ministerial training at Olivet Nazarene College, Kankakee, Ill.

science of aging. This science is frantically trying to keep up with the task of preparing society to properly profit from the potential of the "new minority."

Stereotyping Can Be Hazardous to Your Health

The characteristics often ascribed to senior adults are not always accurate. A recent university study, for instance, showed that a group of college young people actually had more traits generally attributed to senility than the older people also studied. They were more neurotic, negative, dissatisfied, socially inept, or unrealistic.

The general public, including the religious community, needs to learn that there is no typical old person. All persons are different, and age does not change this. An older person is said to be essentially what he or she has always been, only more so.

A person is not headstrong, crotchety, gossipy, in poor health, less bright, disinterested in sex, or afraid to live alone just because he has seen 65 summers.

Many older people have been damaged by these stereotypes which were, in effect, a self-fulfilling prophecy. They were molded by them. "At my age I guess I'm supposed to . . ." is a common phrase. The inference is that one is doomed to act and react in a specific way because of his or her age.

The lesson for teachers of older adults is that the "new minority" should be treated with dignity and accepted as whole persons.

Through This Time of Change

Though many of the truisms about aging are being exploded as myths, the fact of change is not denied and is most crucial with this age-group. Adjustment becomes a way of life. Reality demands it.

It generally begins with the loss of jobs and the status and social contact which goes with them. This often becomes the prelude for a succession of interrelated changes which can be traumatic and devastating.

There is a changing of roles within the home. Homebound husbands frequently complicate household functions. Often, wives decide to take outside jobs to supplement income and to compensate for the empty nest and the feeling of frustration and uselessness.

Physiological changes are inevitable. In a normal course of life, these changes are gradual. In the middle years, sight and hearing deficiencies may occur. The skin wrinkles and hair turns gray—all indications of the aging process.

In the event of strokes, heart disease, diabetes, cancer, and other physical ills, the changes are more drastic. These require radical treatment and may result in permanent impairment and changes in life-style.

It is necessary to see age-related changes as normal and acceptable. It is to be neither pitied nor delayed. The educational climate of the Sunday school can provide a vehicle for learning to live with change, to accept it when it comes, and to allow for changes in others.

The Christian community must not only promote the idea of happy and useful retirement, it must produce happy retired persons who exemplify the concept.

Personhood and Personal Growth

Teachers of senior adults should help their students face candidly such questions as "Who am I?" and "Where am I going?" These often unspoken quandaries do not resolve themselves. They must be dealt with squarely. The need to accept one's age, with its accompanying changes and new involvements, is the basis of living with reality.

The church's (and society's) preoccupation with the youth culture is destined to wane as the population steadily grows older, but immediate steps toward ministering to today's senior adults is a present-tense *must*. This ministry should begin with a two-way acceptance. Youth is the time to begin preparation for the mature years. If they accept it as the normal progression, it will not only prepare them personally for their own aging, but also make mature persons acceptable to them now. Accepting one's own aging—and being accepted by one's contemporaries—is essential to reality and a sense of one's own worth.

Acceptance is accomplished in the educational ministry of the church every time opportunities to learn and participate are provided for senior adults and/or shared with them. Many programs now offered by the church could be modified and extended to include the senior adult. Generational interaction (now viewed by some as the only recourse to offset the deficiencies of the one-generation family)and its support systems should not be reserved for youth and young adults alone.

Personal growth in many areas is possible. Senior adults especially need spiritual guidance. Concepts learned earlier have to be relearned and/or reapplied to present situations. The unspoken assumptions that maturity (age-wise) on the basis of earlier religious experience brings unquenchable faith, undeniable wisdom, and unflagging zeal and devotion is more ideal than real. Suddenly, new trials of faith replace the old. Different temptations occur. New tests of personal commitment, heretofore undreamed of, come into focus. The need for new understanding of spiritual concepts and Bible truths become apparent. No one needs to be more aware of this than Sunday school teachers, adult supervisors, and program planners.

Enrichment Programs for Older Adult Needs

Efforts to focus the Sunday school lesson on mature adult needs is an assignment which requires teaching skill. "What does this scripture have to say to older people?" is a valid question. Or perhaps the question should be "How can an older person put this scripture to practical use?" The alert teacher will constantly make such applications and adaptations in preparing weekly Sunday school lessons.

Guidance for personal Bible study and the organization of Bible study groups can add measurably to the spiritual growth of senior adults. Bible study can and should take on greater significance through these methods at a time when it is greatly needed.

Greater use of church libraries would also enhance the growth of senior adults. While a depth of applicable reading for older people did not exist earlier, there is now a steady stream of new books and periodicals coming to the market beamed to the retiree and the pre-retiree.

On the group level, an education director would be wise to provide classes which deal with image making (and image breaking) for senior adults. Such subjects as grooming, courtesy and mannerisms, mental attitudes, health and nutrition, preretirement preparation, for which many splendid prepared courses are available, is something every church should consider as an elective or an evening activity. It is an established fact that retirees thrown into inactivity without preparation and forethought fare less well when compared to those who were prepared.

Is Fun Just for the Young?

To augment the teaching ministry, a variety of social and recreational activities for senior adults should be planned.

Fellowship on a social level becomes negligible for many retirees unless the church comes to the rescue. To date, no one has come up with a better device than the old-fashioned lunch or potluck dinner to provide an atmosphere of comradeship. Churches are not wise, perhaps, to finance these programs and contribute to the drift toward patronage. A sense of dignity and worth is important to senior adults. A senior adult fellowship such as "The Jolly Sixties" and "The Keen Agers" can be home base for many good programs and ministries involving senior adults.

Image and usefulness can be enhanced by social and recreational activities. Role adjustments and retirement acceptance are involved in recreational programs involving the peer group. A retired person may learn to accept his leisure status if he sees others accepting it and enjoying it, too.

Friendly visiting, Home Department, Sunday school visitation, personal evangelism, and a wide range of volunteer services can be promoted and implemented through an active fellowship with dynamic leaders. Personnel for tasks ranging all the way from administration of business to baby-sitting in the church nursery can be had through this channel. Some exciting Sunday school teachers, children's church leaders, efficient ushers, and experienced planners can be overlooked if age enters the decision.

Discover Needs

Various devices can be used to ascertain the specific needs and interests of mature persons. Unless some method for discovering the needs and interests of these people is utilized, the planners are faced with the possibility of deciding on programs and approaches no one wants, needs, or appreciates. Input from mature persons is the answer to this need.

A church can devise its own questionnaires such as a "Needs and Interests Survey." This can be anonymous, which generally assures more detailed information. General questions relative to age, sex, marital status, church attendance, problem areas, spiritual interests, community activities, service projects, talents, hobbies, travel, sports, leisure-time activities, etc., can be reproduced so that the respondent needs only check the proper place.

A similar method can be used for enumerating opportunities for service through the church and ascertaining interest in these areas. Enlistment devices are needed to locate volunteer services which are in harmony with a person's abilities and concerns.

When enlistment devices and service-opportunity implements do not produce the needed response, the approach might be training sessions. Reluctance to participate is often related to a lack of self-confidence and preparation.

Look Around for Resources

Search for resources beyond your regular Christian education program to complete your planning with and for the "new minority" representatives in your charge. Some helpful books include:

Retirement Is What You Make it, D. Shelby Corlett (Kansas City: Beacon Hill Press of Kansas City, 1973).

Welcome Retirement, Elmer Otte (St. Louis: Concordia, 1974).

Fill Your Days with Life, Mildred Vandenburg (Glendale, Calif.: Regal Books, 1975).

Alive and Past 65, Franklin Seger (Nashville: Broadman Press, 1975).

Senior Adult Ministries with Brother Sam, Sam

Stearman (Kansas City: Beacon Hill Press of Kansas City, 1974).

Investigate community helps. These are sometimes found in local senior citizens' centers, in offices of aging (city, county, state, and federal), and in churches which have established programs for mature adults. Have a look at what others are doing.

The National Council on Aging, and the American Association of Retired Persons (AARP) are among the national groups providing resources for understanding and working with older adults.

The library is always a good source of information, too. Films from religious film distributors now have some very informative and moving productions. Most church offices have catalogues of these sources in their files. Your denominational headquarters welcomes requests for specific information regarding senior adult ministries.

In closing—a challenge. It is a challenge to workers with older adults to help them shed the label "the new minority" in favor of a reputation as the new force for Christ.

Part 2
FOUNDATIONS FROM WHICH WE TEACH

Chapter 6

Stand Here

A Theology for Adult Christian Education

Oscar F. Reed

"Why should I study anything theological?" a Sunday school teacher once said to me. "My hands are full teaching the love of God and the reality of Jesus Christ to my students. I have no time to chatter about theology." What Valerie did not know was that she was a theologian already. Every Sunday morning she was teaching theology.

We are all theologians because we are all asking the same questions about God, Christ, man, experience, and human destiny. Whether it is a teacher of beginners concerned with the love of the Heavenly Father or an open group of young adults pondering a Christian life-style, theology is inevitable.

Because theology is inevitable, every church school teacher should be aware of his theological presuppositions

---

OSCAR F. REED is professor of philosophy of religion and Christian ethics at Nazarene Theological Seminary. Formerly he was chairman of the Division of Religion at Pasadena College and at Bethany Nazarene College.

He holds degrees from Bethany Nazarene College (A.B., Th.B.) and the University of Southern California (M.Th., Ph.D.).

Dr. Reed's writings include "Amos," "Joel," and "Hosea" in *Beacon Bible Commentary* and "1 and 2 Corinthians" in the *Beacon Bible Expositions* series. He has also served 16 years as a pastor.

and how they enter into the fabric of teaching. If he isn't, his educational principles will dictate to his theology rather than his theology act as a guide to his educational philosophy.

Some have spoken of an educational strategy without any theology, but such is a caricature. Education always has a theology. The issue is not the fact of theology, but what kind of theology. The last few years have produced a shift from a psychological to a theological environment. And while the movement has many times been too swift and painless, resulting in "superficial theologizing," it has made Christian educators aware of the demand of a relationship between education and theology. The secular mood of our society demands the same of all evangelicals.

What Is Christian Theology?

John MacQuarrie has defined Christian theology as having "to do with the unfolding and elucidation [clarification] of the knowledge of God that is given to us in the revelation of Jesus Christ."[1] That knowledge is a unique kind of knowledge, for God is not a thing to be identified or an object to be discovered. The knowledge of God comes from a communion with Him.

A dynamic theology cannot rest with a knowledge *about* God, and it positively abhors a chattering concerning God. Knowledge *of* God, like knowledge of our friends, must finally be a knowledge based on communion. We must always remember, however, that God is greater than our knowledge of Him. It is idolatry to think that we have known God in His fullness. He is neither a fact "out there" nor an exalted ideal "in here." He can possess us through His Holy Spirit, but we can never possess Him. "God transcends anything we can grasp or contain and when we think we have him, the truth is that he has slipped through our grasp and we are left clinging to some pitiful idol of our making. We can never know God by seeking to grasp and manipulate him, but only by letting him grasp us."[2]

Although we "see in part," it is the task of theology to systematize human knowledge about God, man, sin, salvation, and human destiny. It is the task of Christian education to impart this knowledge.

Theology in Context

The commonest error of the Christian educator is to allow the strands of theology, worship, and action to become separated. The three are triple-born. If we allow the strands to divide, the isolation of any one will weaken the other two. Isolation was already criticized in the New Testament when James confronted the Jewish Christians with: "You believe that God is one; you do well. Even the demons believe—and shudder" (2:19, RSV).

There are many teachers who would either reject or ignore theological sensitivities to settle in on worship (celebration) and life (Christian ethics) when both presuppose a theology which make their interpretation possible. There are no shortcuts from the faith of the gospel and the acting out of that faith in "daily deeds of self-giving love."

Christian theology is a part of the total fabric of the Christian religion. It is not an expression of the ivory tower, but of the sanctuary, the schoolroom, and the marketplace. It can only be appreciated within the context of the whole. If isolated, theology becomes distorted and will wither away and die. It is because of this unity that Christian education can only make sense in a theological setting. This chapter is not written to suggest a theology of Christian education, but a Christian theology from which education can emerge as a living arm of the community of faith.

The chief source of theology for the whole church is the Bible. While there may be some freedom in interpreting the Bible, the evangelical branches of Christianity all believe that the Bible is the chief Authority. We are thus faced with the relevance of biblical theology for Christian education.

Christian education, then, is in need of some structure and method of interpreting the message of the Bible and how to communicate that message to adults of differing ages and degrees of awareness. The rest of this chapter is given to the basic beliefs that a teacher of adults should understand and make his own. He should stand here. These basic doctrines should serve as a foundation. They should determine his stance in the crosswinds of ideas. Notions, whims, and insights should all be tested by how they harmonize or conflict with these foundational beliefs.

God's Self-disclosure

At the heart of the Christian faith is God who has taken the initiative to disclose himself to us in His Son Jesus Christ, to which the Bible is witness.[3]

The Bible tells a story. It is a proclamation of God's good news, beginning with the Creation Hymn and continuing through to the Revelation of Jesus Christ. It is the story of "a people" who become the vehicle of God's revelation. As Randolph Miller puts it, "It begins with what God has done and proceeds to imply who He is. It is a record of events, of God's acts on the stage of history and of man's response to God. It is the story of personal relationships between a divine personal being and human persons. The chief actor in this historical drama is God."[4]

At the beginning of Christian theology is a faith in God's self-disclosure—eternally creative, continually acting and seeking to bring men into right relationship with

Him through the Personal Word as revealed in the written Word. God's work is progressive both in revelation and inspiration. He accepts a primitive culture and calls a "no people" to be "His people." He establishes a covenant with Abraham, Jacob, and Moses, looking forward to the new covenant established in Jesus Christ.

The Holy Scriptures demonstrate the story of God at work in history. It is the record of relationships in which men in their willfulness sinned and could not of themselves effect a reconciliation.

Miller suggests that the biblical drama may be divided into five acts:

I. Creation
II. Covenant
III. Christ
IV. Church
V. Consummation.[5]

We live in Act IV, with the work of the Holy Spirit in His Church under the lordship of Christ. The glorious hope of Christ's advent is still to come, when His judgment in the end times will make all things right.

The Incarnate God

Jesus the Christ is the suffering Servant of God incarnate in God's unique Son.[6]

In Jesus Christ is the "Word became flesh." In Him we see what a human life can be. He lived our life, suffered our temptations, was misunderstood and tragically misinterpreted. Finally He was crucified and laid in the tomb of Joseph. This was not the Messiah that the Jews had expected, and they rejected Him on that count rather than on His prophetic mission.

But for the Christian, Christ was the Fulfillment of Old Testament prophecy. He was the "suffering servant" of Isaiah and the virgin-born, Bethlehem Babe expected in Micah. He is raised by the power of God the third day to stand at the right hand of God and to live in our hearts forever. He is the living Christ. In Him was the new covenant written in the blood of the Saviour and the beginning of the New Israel in Christ.

The whole motive for existence is now found in God's Son, our Saviour, Jesus Christ. He is the Hope and the Dynamic of our life as expressed through His Church. In His obedience to the Father we find a model for our obedience through Him to the Father.

The Holy Spirit

The Holy Spirit is the Third Person of the Triune God who is ever present and active in Christ's Church, personally witnessing to the truth that is in Jesus Christ.[7]

The Holy Spirit is God. This needs to be stated clearly again and again. The failure to state it fully leads to many false conceptions. The Holy Spirit is the almighty Creator of heaven and earth, who was revealed in the fullness of His nature and power in the person of Jesus Christ, and who now claims our human existence as His chosen and rightful dwelling place. "The Holy Spirit is God in that form of his being in which he is able to be the life-giving center of countless human lives."[8] He is not a vague influence, or a mode of fellowship, or a "something" that "breathes" through the universe, but a personal wellspring of life—God himself. Everything that can be said about God the Father and Jesus Christ His Son can also be said of the Holy Spirit.

The work of the Holy Spirit is the actualizing of God's sovereign power through Jesus Christ, breaking in upon the lives of persons and invading the world through the community of believers—the Church. It is in the fellowship of the Holy Spirit where God comes closest to us in sovereign power and grace. He is the Spirit of Christ. Whatever we find in Christ we discover in Him. He is involved in all Christian teaching and learning. We can do nothing apart from Him.

The Holy Spirit will rebuke self-idolatry and legalism. His coming is always on invitation: "Come, Holy Spirit, I pray." We can enter into the holy pilgrimage and point others to the Way in the joyful hope of God's coming in the power of the Spirit.

The Reality of Sin

We, God's creatures, have broken our fellowship with Him because we have followed our own way and in sin are depraved—an estrangement and alienation from our essential nature which can only be resolved in grace.[9]

Sin is far more than the serious offences that men commit against God's laws and society. The story of the fall of man in the third chapter of Genesis, the parable of the prodigal son, and Paul's letter to the Romans all speak of a universal tragedy from which no man is spared—"All have sinned, and come short of the glory of God" (Rom. 3: 23). When Eve said, "I know better than God knows for me," she was expressing the universal rebellion against a life of fellowship with God.

When man, then, became the center of his own existence and was cut apart from God, his humanity became broken, wounded, and disordered. In this respect, salvation becomes the promise of man's essential humanity as exhibited in Jesus Christ.

The authentic expression of man's sinfulness is not his disgraceful or antisocial conduct, but simply his self-centeredness—a self-idolatry which is the very heart of sin. We have chosen our own way and in the choosing have determined to follow our own desires instead of God's will in Christ.

The disorder of sin is first in man himself. He is in contradiction to himself and so in tension with himself. Paul calls this being "carnally minded," which is "enmity against God," for it can be no other.

It is only when we see this depth dimension in sin that we can see the profound meaning of redemption.

The Christian teacher of adults cannot view human nature as neutral with certain potentials. He must understand the brokenness of human existence, which is universal to all men.

The Good News of Full Salvation

The good news is that Christ through His death and resurrection bridged the alienation between God and man, making provision for our salvation and holy obedience to God.[10]

Only when we see the reality of sin can we begin to understand the miracle of forgiveness. That forgiveness is offered to all men who repent and believe. It is far more than a moralism—doing what is right in our own strength. Salvation includes the reconciliation and renewal of the whole man. The forgiveness that Christ offered is not a "cheap grace," but one which carries with it an expected response of obedience in faith. The forgiven is accepted into the fellowship of God, a restoration to the relationship which sin forfeited, and an introduction into a life of obedience resulting in infinite richness.

The purpose of Jesus' coming was to "save his people from their sins." It is here that Paul and Luther express their trust in justification by faith (alone). The sinner is redeemed, not by works, but by God's acceptance of him in

Jesus Christ. Righteousness is not what man achieves—it is a "gift of God."

We can come to God because God has first come to us in Jesus Christ. "Jesus Christ is God's invasion of our humanity to conquer the sin that holds it prisoner and perverts it into inhumanity, and the weapon of His conquest is His infinitely forgiving love."

The place of love's decisive victory over sin was Calvary. The Cross was Jesus' final giving of himself to us and for us. When Christ forgives, it is an assurance that the undeserving sinner has been accepted in love because Christ took that sin and bore it on the Cross. We are accepted because of what He has done!

The forgiveness of Christ gives us an awareness of our own sinfulness and the need for the cleansing power of God in entire sanctification. The sanctifying presence of God is given and in process from the moment of acceptance. But there comes a time and moment when we take the second step within the full scope of redemption. Here is the impossible possibility—the wonder of divine paradox.

Paul clearly saw this imperative after recognizing in Romans 6 that those who are in Christ are *dead to sin* and *no longer slaves to sin.* He follows that marvelous witness by appealing to the Romans *to present* themselves *to God as slaves for obedience, to present themselves as slaves of righteousness, resulting in sanctification.*

Paul in Rom. 12:1 and 1 Thess. 5:23-24 appeals to his converts to fill out the offerings of divine love in perfect obedience resulting in sanctification. In the latter passage, the promise is that the experience of entire sanctification leading to holy obedience actualizes the promise of forgiveness in Christ and the glorious hope to come. And while analogies always fall short, the pilgrimage is not divided into different categories but moments of crisis in action within the total scope of salvation. Perfect love is the catalyst that makes the continuing pilgrimage possible.

While the cleansing from sin is the negative aspect of sanctification, perfect love is the positive result of the crisis within the life in Christ. Wesley is on good ground when he interprets the perfection of the New Testament as a fullness of love and grace. Undoubtedly, the ideal to which we are called is a life of love for our God and our neighbor, so filled with the Spirit that pride and selfishness have no room. It is "love expelling sin."

The whole drive toward Christian holiness is not an agonizing effort to achieve personal purity, but a commitment to God's purpose until purity of intention is the result. That is why the key word in Romans 6 and 12:1 is the verb "present" ("present your bodies"). The Christian is called to "seek first," not his own purity, but the "total reign of God." When we finally give allegiance to the total lordship of Christ, we *are* pure. That vertical expression of our relationship to God is now revealed through our horizontal concern for our neighbor.

Service and Fellowship in the Church

We find our fellowship and opportunity for service through the Church, the community of saints, the body of Christ of which Christ is the continuing, incarnate Head.[11]

When God speaks His Word to us and we hear that Word, we become God's men and the servant of God's Word—the channel through which it may be heard by other men. There is never a Word of God without a people of God "living under the judgment and by the promise of that word and by their very existence bearing witness to the reality of God before all men."[12] If we believe in the Holy

Trinity of God, we must believe in the Universal Church as the body of Christ.

Interestingly enough, until recently, there have been few Protestant churches that have given any real space to the doctrine of the Church and its history in their educational programs. There must be a place in our creed for the existence and understanding of the Church.

James D. Smart points out that "we must be careful to distinguish between loyalty to the church, or enthusiasm for it or even love for it, and belief in it as an article of faith in close and inseparable association with our belief in God."[13]

The origin of the Church is not human, but divine. The Church was necessary for the unfolding of God's purpose in the midst of men. The whole purpose of God was for "a people" to receive the Word in covenant in order that they might be committed to a mission. The Israel of the Old Testament is a foreshadowing of the Church. The New Testament is the New Israel under the new covenant in Christ. Its reality is in the person of Jesus Christ.

To think that one can live apart from the Church as a Christian is a serious error. To receive the Holy Spirit is to bind one's spirit in oneness with all who have confessed Christ throughout all the ages. It immediately becomes apparent why a Christian educator *must* include the idea of the Church in his theological creed. And while a particular church may in some respects be unfaithful to its nature (Corinth, for example), yet it is God's Church and exists by God's grace in spite of its sin and unfaithfulness.

A New Testament definition of the Church will help us to understand its true nature. The New Testament knew nothing of individual faith apart from covenant community. The love of Christ led to a genuine fellowship *(koinonia)*.

While there are a number of descriptive terms of the

Church in the New Testament, the most vivid and familiar is the "body of Christ" of which Christ is the Head.[14] This idea reveals the mutual support which Christians have for each other in deep unity with Christ.

The Christian Hope

We stand within the circle of the Church under the direction of the Holy Spirit, looking in hope to "that day" when the kingdom of God shall be fulfilled.[15]

The Christian life is an affirmation that our hope is not in the things which are seen, but the things which are unseen. The resurrection of Jesus Christ must be understood as the "decisive relation of the primacy and power of the unseen world of God in the midst of this world which is marked by the sign of death."[16] Therefore, the communion with the living Lord in His Church is set over against death. When the Church saw its Source of life in the reality of Jesus Christ, it was transformed and empowered to invade the world in spite of that world.

> It dare not be forgotten that the church that expected Christ's return at any moment was a church in which to be Christian was to be unconditionally open to the presence and power of the Spirit who was the Spirit of Christ. The joy of Christians in which they knew of Christ in the Spirit made them impatient to know him face to face.[17]

Eternal life, then, does not stand in antithesis to death, but a life shared with Christ through His Spirit. Death is the final enemy, but the resurrection of the body is the authentic hope of every follower of Jesus Christ.

Faith is not faith about Jesus Christ, but faith in Him, a trust that our life in Him, both in life and in death, can be crowned only in the final triumph of that union. It is only in this oneness with Jesus Christ, and our death to self because of His death, that we can believe in the resurrection of the body and life everlasting.

Affirmations of Our Faith

The seven affirmations of faith form the doctrinal foundation on which adult teachers must stand. They form the heart of the Christian faith. Fads, methodologies, and tangents will rise, but the fads will fade and the anchors of the faith will still remain. The Christian teacher must be sure that he anchors his ministry in the permanent affirmations of faith, not in "every wind of doctrine," lest his ministry fade with the fads.

Chapter 7

Toward a Philosophy for Adult Christian Education

A Theology/Philosophy for Teachers of Adults

Donald S. Metz

Contemporary philosophy represents a riches-to-rags story. At one time the realm of philosophy claimed sovereignty over practically the entire range of thought. Like the cattlemen of the Old West, philosophers regarded the vast plains of intellectual grazing as their particular territory. But along came academic sheriffs, scientific sodbusters, and psychological sheepherders. Philosophy was forced to reduce its range. Academic areas such as astronomy, physics, psychology, and sociology gradually fenced off their own ranges and became distinctive endeavors.

DONALD S. METZ is executive editor of the Department of Church Schools, Church of the Nazarene. He holds degrees from Eastern Nazarene College (A.B.), the University of Maryland (M.A.), Lancaster Theological Seminary (B.D.), Southwestern Baptist Theological Seminary (D.R.E.), and the University of Oklahoma (Ph.D.).

Dr. Metz served 12 years as a pastor before joining the faculty at Bethany Nazarene College, where he taught for 16 years. From 1965 to 1974, he served as academic dean at Mid-America Nazarene College. Dr. Metz has written several books, including *Speaking in Tongues* and *Studies in Biblical Holiness*. He was also a contributor to *Beacon Bible Commentary*.

Philosophy still claims homesteader rights, however, to the basic areas of what is real, how we know, what are values, how we relate ideas, and what is beauty. And while education frequently attempts to pioneer in lands untrammeled by philosophy, the bid ends in failure. Education is inextricably linked to philosophy.

But before we begin to build a philosophy for adult Christian education, we must review our priorities. While secular education starts with philosophy as the foundation stone, Christian education regards theological affirmations as the primary foundation. Philosophy begins with man, extends itself to include ultimate reality, and comes to rest again on a human base. Theology begins with God, reaches out to embrace man and his world, and returns to God. Theology is God-centered. Philosophy is man-centered.

Thus for the Christian educator, a theology of education precedes a philosophy of education. Philosophy of education may be defined as *the application of a particular set of rational concerns to the theory and practice of the teaching-learning process.* A theology of education may be defined as *the application of a church's doctrine to its educational theory and practice.*

Since the Christian believes revelation more important than humanistic rationality, the priority of theology is established.

Foundational Theological Affirmations

The theological beliefs of a group bear an essential relationship to the objectives, to the curriculum content, and to the methodology of Christian education. Therefore, without indulging in needless repetition of the previous chapter, let us proceed to briefly posit our theological affirmations. The following doctrines present a minimal list of biblical teachings which form the solid core of the educational work of adult Christian education.

Biblical revelation. The Bible is the inspired Record of God's redemptive revelation to mankind. The Bible is the Word of God, revealed to spiritually sensitive men through the illumination of the Holy Spirit. It speaks with final authority in all matters of personal redemption, spiritual faith, and moral duty. The Bible has meaning for all ages and for all ethnic groups.

The Lord God Almighty. The God of the Christian faith steps into life as the everlasting I AM of history. God structured the universe and, as the Creator, brought man into existence. As Sovereign, God sustains the totality of all that is and directs the stream of life toward a grand climax.

Jesus the Christ. Jesus Christ is the eternal Son of God, coequal with the Father, and is the Saviour of mankind. As the Son of Man, he was God incarnate, the promised Messiah, the present Redeemer. Christ is our Example of righteousness, our inspired Teacher of truth, our Criterion of service, our voluntary Sacrifice on the Cross, our resurrected Lord, and our coming King.

The Holy Spirit. The Holy Spirit is a Person, a Center of self-conscious awareness and activity, One with the Father and the Son. He is the instrumental Agent in salvation. The Holy Spirit achieves in man personal, subjective regeneration; continual spiritual growth; and experiential sanctification. The Holy Spirit sustains and directs the Christian.

Man. Man was created by God in His own image. Christian education differs radically from secular education in regarding man as an immortal soul, as a being sinful by nature, and as a being of infinite worth and dignity. Man is free to choose his destiny. Man is helpless to save himself and is utterly dependent on divine grace. Man possesses the capacity for spiritual response, faith, and complete transformation through redemption in Christ.

Sin. Sin is a reality in human life. Sin is not mere separation, ignorance, or weakness. Sin is both an act of the will and a state of spiritual corruption. It is a broken relationship and a subjective imbalance. The essence of sin is rebellion, idolatry, and self-love. Sin separates man from God, corrupts the will, mind, emotions, and imagination—the total person. Sin brings the condemnation of God. The sole method of freeing one from sin is through the love and forgiveness of God through faith in Christ.

Salvation. Salvation comes as the free gift of God through faith in Christ. Salvation includes a subjective regeneration and a new relationship. Salvation actually begins with the working of grace in the life of a sinner. Christian conversion initiates one into the family of God and the fellowship of the church. Salvation ends when a person stands in heaven before God as a redeemed soul.

Christian Growth. The Christian life includes both crises and process. The two distinctive crises are regeneration and entire sanctification. Evangelism emphasizes the two climactic experiences in the Christian life. Christian education concerns itself primarily with growth and development. The Christian life is neither *static* nor *dynamic*—it grows continually and naturally. Growth is not automatic. Education offers help in developing spiritual knowledge and understanding in fostering Christlike attitudes, appreciations, and loyalties, and in nourishing patterns of worship and service.

The Mission of the Church. The Church was founded by divine initiative and stands as the body of Christ. The church is both organization and organism. As an organization, the church operates according to stated polity and within specific guidelines. As an organism, the Church lives in the fellowship of believers and the expressions of mission in the world.

The World Order. The present world order presents a confused, even a dismaying picture. From the biblical point of view, this world order is under the dominion of Satan. Christian education seeks to alleviate the world situation even when the task appears hopeless. Christians assume the stance of being the salt of the earth and the light of the world.

Last Things. The Christian view of history is not evolutional and naturalistic. Christian education regards history's course as purposeful and redemptive. Human history began at the dawn of creation. This phase of human history as we know it will close with the consummation known as the second coming of Christ. The final note for the Christian is hope perfected in love and unending life in a limitless heaven.

Toward a Philosophy for Adult Christian Education

After nailing down the preceding theological affirmations, the Christian educator can move into the area of philosophy. A philosophy of education offers a specific set of principles and values for the various areas of education. While the "given" for Christian education comes from theology, philosophy may be utilized as a bridge between the church and secular education. A philosophy of education when presented by the church is the church interpreting its educational process in the language of human reason. Philosophy also may serve an evaluative function regarding the consistency between theory and practice in Christian education. Finally, philosophy maintains a concern for precise use of language which Christian education could emulate with advantage.

Classical philosophical theory revolves around the following pivotal problems: (1) *metaphysics*—the question of ultimate reality; (2) *epistemology*—deals with the nature of knowledge and how one knows what is true; (3) *axiology*—studies the essence of values and value systems, or what is right and wrong; (4) *logic*—deals with relationship of ideas and correct reasoning; (5) *aesthetics*—the discussion of beauty and harmony, as related to the sources, forms, and effects of art. The following discussion is limited to metaphysics, epistemology, and axiology, for they are of prime concern to Christian education.

The Metaphysics of Christian Education

The metaphysics (theory of reality) of adult Christian education is *God-centered* and *nature-related*.

God-centered. To the Christian, God is the ultimate Reality. The Bible makes no attempt to prove the existence of God. Philosophical reasons (arguments) may be used to support a belief in God. But the existence of God is the starting point of all Christian endeavor. It is the unprovable and assumed presupposition of Christian life and thought. Christian education which is truly biblical begins, proceeds, and ends with the reality of the Triune God.

Nature-related. Christian thinking accepts also the reality of nature as God's creation. Such a view is admittedly a type of dualism. But the dualism is complimentary rather than antagonistic. Nature may be called a secondary reality and God the primary Reality.

From this point of view, God and nature are inextricably bound together. A God-centered and nature-related concept of reality is in harmony with the Old Testament teachings when nature is regarded as the handiwork of God.

A God-centered and nature-related metaphysics has direct implications for both the objectives, the content, and the methodology of Christian education.

If we accept God as an exclusive Reality, then we may be in the area of personalistic idealism. Philosophical idealists tend to stress the development of the intellect by the traditional methods of memorization, lecture, etc. Stress is placed on the deductive method of learning. If we accept nature as an exclusive reality, we find ourselves in some type of reductionistic naturalism. Philosophical naturalists usually emphasize personal or social development by such methods as projects, interaction groups, and other activities. The inductive method is used, and students are guided from the concrete to the abstract, from the specific to the general.

If we accept a God-centered, nature-related metaphysics, then the educational approach incorporates both traditional and progressive ideas and methods.

The Epistemology of Christian Education

Epistemology deals with the nature of knowledge and the problem of how one knows what is true. For the Christian, there is ultimate truth, even though finite man cannot fully understand infinite truth. Christian education points to several sources of knowledge, including revelation, reason, nature, and human experience.

Revelation as a Source of Knowledge. The Bible is the Focal Point of Christian epistemology. Accepting the biblical Revelation as true is admittedly an act of faith. In reality, accepting any source of knowledge as valid is an act of faith. In the biblical approach, Jesus stands as "the Truth."

Christian education does not use the Bible primarily as a Textbook. Textbooks may be studied aside from personal involvement, for factual data is the primary consideration. But the Bible is a Book of life. Only those who share the life described and prescribed in the Bible possess the ability to understand the spiritual relevance of the Word.

Reason as a Source of Knowledge. The role of reason in Christian knowledge varies from a depreciation of reason to an exaltation of reason. In the Wesleyan tradition, reason holds a highly respected, but not an ultimately authoritative, role. John Wesley taught that reason was a part of man's inherent nature and should not be despised. Reason is thus able to offer partial or supportive truth—but not ultimate truth.

Nature as a Source of Knowledge. The God of nature cannot contradict the God of divine revelation. The facts of science cannot contradict the truth of the Bible. The assumptions of science may often conflict with the presumptions of religion. Natural revelation pictures the physical wonders of the universe in their beauty and complexity. While nature bears overwhelming evidence to God and His greatness, it does not reveal His love or impart knowledge of eternal life.

Experience as a Source of Knowledge. Experience contributes to one's knowledge of God and man. The experiences of biblical characters and the witness of numberless Christians point to truth. Human experience, however, must always submit to biblical approval.

The Axiology of Christian Education

The problem reviewed in axiology is the problem of values. Such questions as the good and the bad, the evil and the beneficial, the permanency or temporary nature of values comprise the arena of debate. The current popularity of existential ideas presents a challenge to Christian thinking. The following statements offer an abbreviated approach to Christian axiology.

Christian values are Christ-centered. Since Christ stands as the everlasting Reference Person, He becomes the ultimate Source of a scale of values.

Christian values are eternity-oriented. A Christian lives in two worlds at one time. In the midst of a materialistic culture, Christian education attempts to inculcate a system of values having its destiny in heaven.

Christian values are person-related. Man represents God's most noble creation. Created in God's image, man deserves respect, love, and understanding. Even though marred by sin, man yet stands tall among the creatures of the earth. Values that are Christ-centered find their finest expression in interpersonal relationships.

Christian values are Spirit-directed. The Holy Spirit is the great Sensitizer. He continually prods us and alerts us in our development as Christians.

In expressing its bipolar nature, Christian education begins with theology. Theological concepts produce both the architectural design and the building materials of Christian education. Philosophical analysis helps to balance Christian education with human patterns of thought and life. A philosophy of education applies the language of disciplined thought to educational processes. A theology of education uses the language of faith to make a practical application of essential doctrines to the educational work of the church. Thus the working philosophy of education for adult Christian education becomes a theological philosophy or a theology/philosophy of education properly so called.

Part 3
PRACTICS FOR TEACHERS

Chapter 8

When Jesus Taught the Adult Class

A Look at the Teaching Methods of Jesus

Wesley Tracy

Don't tell me—let me guess! You blew it again, right? Such a tremendous Sunday school lesson, and you just simply couldn't get a thing across.

"I try—I try. This morning I presented the material the best I could. I asked three really pertinent questions, and all I got was eight blank stares, one snicker, and a snore. I think I'm going to..."

If this sounds familiar, perhaps what you need to do is go back to square one and take a long look at the Master Teacher at work.

Jesus Came Teaching

Jesus knew all about teaching. Every principle that educational psychologists and specialists have unearthed over the last 2,000 years, Jesus already knew. You can't learn everything you need to know about teaching by reading the rather skimpy accounts of Jesus the Teacher. But you can learn a lot.

It would be worse than useless to try to duplicate the exact teaching situations in which Jesus taught. It would be rather tough to buckle your students into a time machine and regress to a pastoral scene in the Judean hills.

Think how funny you would look standing on a boat in your Sunday suit with your class sitting in the sand of a Sea of Galilee beach. A prayerful study of Jesus the Teacher, nevertheless, will give your teaching new significance.

Whatever else may be said of Jesus, He was a *teacher*. Though some dimensions of the nature of the God-man may have to be filed under "Mystery," there is no doubt that He was a teacher. He called himself a teacher. He accepted that label from others. Even His enemies called Him "Teacher." His disciples seldom called Him anything else. Ninety-seven times the New Testament refers to His activity as teaching.

Jesus the Teacher came into a society encrusted with the legalistic formalism of Judaism. "His matchless message and dynamic teaching burst through the hard crust of the religious traditionalism that had engulfed the Jewish people and fanned the smoldering ember of their faith until it became a living fire."[1]

The teaching of Jesus has influenced history. As C. B. Eavey observes, "His teachings had no human source.... He came from God and He taught God's message.... He taught as God, 'as one having authority.' Everything He taught He exemplified in His actions. Jesus was before He did, He lived what He taught, and lived it before He taught it."[2]

The Master's Methods

Variety was the keynote of Jesus' teaching. Discussion, lecture, drama, question and answer, field trips, demonstrations, and projects were in His teaching repertoire. In addition, He added punch and sparkle to His teaching by making frequent use of visual aids.

Question and Answer. In few other areas does the teaching skill of Jesus shine forth so brilliantly as in His mastery of the question-and-answer method. He used direct questions, indirect questions, and hypothetical questions.

Though modern educators shun the *direct question* like poison ivy, Jesus realized that it had value in that it elicited information.

Thus Jesus asked a demoniac, "What is your name?" The answer was "Legion," which communicated truth both to the Framer of the question and to the respondent. Jesus asked a sick man, "Do you want to be healed?" At other times He asked sick persons something like this: "Do you believe I am able to do this?" Occasionally Jesus used the direct question to answer a question (Mark 10:2-3).

Sometimes Jesus used an *indirect question* to prod people to productive thinking. His question "What think ye of Christ?" (Matt. 22:41) sparked meaningful thought and discussion.

Jesus frequently used the *hypothetical question*. Stating an imaginary situation (parable or example), He would ask for thoughtful analysis and interpretation.[3]

It is interesting that the first recorded words of Jesus as a boy are in the form of a question (Luke 2:49). When He called His first disciples, He initiated the conversation with a question, "What seek ye?" His question gave the two courage to make an inquiry of their own. The result was that "they . . . abode with him that day" (John 1:38-39). At the close of His ministry, Jesus was still using questions. On the morning of the Resurrection, Mary stood by the tomb, crying her heart out. The risen Lord could have proclaimed His resurrection. But instead He asked two questions: "Woman, why are you weeping? Whom are you seeking?"[4]

During one *question and answer* session, Jesus used a visual tool to get the point across when words alone could not. The questions and answers revolved around the enforcement of the Mosiac law on adultery. A woman, guilty of that sin, was present. The law said that she was to be stoned to death. Jesus' words, "He that is without sin . . . first cast a stone," failed to communicate to them that divine mercy, not Mosaic judgment, was to prevail.

Jesus then resorted to the use of a visual aid. Not having a Magic Marker and flip chart or even a chalkboard handy, He did the next best thing. He wrote in the sand with His finger. We may never know what He wrote, but before the last dusty jot and tittle were formed, the guilty got the message and were gone.

In another *question and answer* encounter, some sharpies tried to *corner the Teacher*. They zeroed in on Him with a loaded question having to do with the secular versus the sacred. With the use of a visual aid, Jesus sprang the trap and clarified the issue for those who really wanted to learn and reduced to consternation those who were trying to disrupt the class. He asked for a coin, and holding it up for all to *see,* he asked, "Whose is this image and superscription?"

"Caesar's," they answered. Whereupon Jesus replied, "Render unto Caesar the things which are Caesar's; and unto God the things that are God's," and dismissed the class.

Demonstration. Tired of telling your class over and over what you mean? Try *showing* them. Use a demonstration to communicate the message. Jesus was a walking Demonstration of what He taught.

Jesus had talked to His class (the 12 disciples) many times about humility. When they desperately needed another lesson on the theme, Jesus did not formulate a scholarly discourse. Rather, He resorted to a demonstration.

As the class gathered for dinner, Jesus sent the slave boy on a coffee break while He himself took up the slave's tools and task. He filled the basin with water, put the towel over His arm, and began to wash the disciples' dusty, aching feet.

His class members never forgot. They never got over it. To their dying day they remembered Christ and His towel.

Field Trips. "Money, money, money! That's all this church ever thinks about." Do such snide remarks make you nervous when you have to teach on stewardship? Maybe it's because you spend too much time lecturing on the subject. One day when the lesson was on giving, Jesus took His whole class on a field trip to show them what giving was all about. He did not harangue them with a loud lecture from Malachi, but marched them into the sanctuary to observe the morning offering.

In those days they did not pass the plates. Instead, they passed the people! That is, the people marched by the offering receptacle and dropped in their gifts. The class watched as the rich men, stroking their beards in sanctimonious satisfaction, put in large amounts from fat purses. They were impressed. But the visual aid that carried the lesson home to their hearts was a poor widow who self-consciously gave two mites—all her living. After the class had seen the real meaning of stewardship, the Teacher had but to summarize the lesson in a few words and send them on their way from a profitable learning session.

Discussion. Do you wish you could make those abstract biblical doctrines understandable? You know how it usually goes. The concepts are not clear-cut, and as a result you get into a discussion that goes off in all directions and leads to nowhere. Once Jesus got into a discussion like that with a woman. His experience illustrates one of the problems with discussion teaching: The discussion often gets off the subject. The Lord wanted to talk with the woman about eternal life, but she kept taking the discussion off in the wrong direction. The conversation covered racial prejudice, the history of Israel, the woman's marital status (or lack of it), and the proper place and mode of worship. Christ, however, used a visual teaching tool to maintain control of the situation and finally get around to eternal life. To help her understand, He called it "living water," and He used the well and her waterpot as visual aids.

The effort proved fruitful, for the Bible says that "many of the Samaritans . . . believed on him for the saying of the woman which testified."

Buzz Groups. Ever try buzz groups? Of course you are right when you say that one of the problems with this technique is that when the groups come back together, their reports are either all the same or scattered and off the subject. If the reports are scattered, it is difficult to pull them together in a meaningful conclusion. If they are the same, you find yourself flailing away at the obvious.

After a buzz group session had gone off in the wrong direction, Jesus used a visual aid to salvage it and make it a beneficial learning experience. Christ had just performed some pretty impressive miracles, and the disciples were really carried away about the coming kingdom of Christ and their respective positions therein. Jesus allowed them to carry on a long and heated buzz group session. The mother of James and John apparently was one of the buzz group leaders. Calling them all together, Jesus took a humble, trusting child in His arms and said, "Except ye . . . become as little children, ye shall not enter into the kingdom of heaven. Whosoever therefore shall humble himself as this little child, the same is the greatest in the kingdom of heaven." The child, a visual aid, got the point across.

Projects. If teachers of adults could see their students putting their lessons to work, most teachers would stop wearing faces that look like clocks at 20 minutes after eight. How about your students? Do they lose a lot in translating your words into their behavior?

Jesus helped His pupils with this problem by involving them in projects. Sometimes Jesus divided His class into teams of two and sent them out in on-the-job training expeditions. You can be sure that these real-world confrontations made the learning experience effective.

Jesus' witnessing teams went a step further than many such modern ventures. When it is left up to us twentieth-century Christians, too often we offer a cram course in witnessing, pour heads full of knowledge *about* witnessing, arm the students with a bibliography, two tracts, and a chart—and never get around to making the witnessing project itself a reality. Jesus knew that people "learn by doing" long before John Dewey stumbled onto the idea on a pensive night in Oil City, Pa.

Drama. Well, you say, maybe Jesus did use those methods, but there's one thing He didn't do. Our supervisor has been nagging at us to use *drama*—that's one thing Jesus didn't use!

Wrong! He did use *drama*. When a distinct lesson was needed on reverence for God's house, Jesus decided that a dramatization would be just the thing to communicate a memorable lesson. What a performance He gave! It was so impressive that Matthew, Mark, Luke, and John all included it in their brief biographies of Christ.

Watch Him as He makes His way through the sellers of doves, and the sellers of lambs, and the money changers. Where did He get those cords? They look like temple drapery cords. His face is clouded with indignation. He asks Peter for a knife. He cuts the cords into three-foot lengths and ties knots in them.

Look! What? He's making something. What could it . . . ? Why are the Good Shepherd's eyes snapping fire?

Yes—that's it. A whip—He's making a whip! Man, is He disturbed! Look out! There go the money changers' tables! Money all over the floor!

Listen to that whip zinging over the heads of the dove sellers! He has opened the dove cages. The sellers are wailing! Why don't the guards do something? But look, there's something about that countenance that makes cowards of us all.

Quiet! He speaks. *"It is written, My house is the house of prayer: but ye have made it a den of thieves."*

No one who attended church that day ever lived long enough to forget the time Jesus came to church. If He had merely made a mild little speech, everyone would have forgotten it by lunchtime.

Storytelling. To write amply about the stories (parables) of Jesus would require volumes. Let us here consider only a few key points.

Jesus showed us a mastery of the art of teaching with stories. He sets the model for modern teachers. His stories are marvels of unity and brevity.

His stories were subjects that were familiar to His hearers—animals, plants, family relations, harvest, travelers, etc.

What Jesus showed us about parables has become an educational law today: "From the concrete to the abstract; from the simple to the complex; from things through symbols to relations."[5] Perhaps the best tip here for today's teacher is: *Explain the abstract in concrete terms.* Jesus did this whether speaking in parables or not. You have heard speakers say things like "Because of the transitory character of human existence, men confused by the human predicament sometimes put their trust in temporal things at the expense of things eternal to their own detriment."

Well, Jesus knew better than to indulge in such abstract double-talk. He expressed the same idea in simple, *concrete* terms: "What shall it profit a man if he gain the whole world and lose his own soul?"

The stories of Jesus have been truly effective. One authority on storytelling says: "The stories of the Gospels have done infinitely more to influence the lives of men than all the books of systematic theology that the church has produced in twenty centuries of time."[6]

Lecture. I've heard some droning lectures in Sunday school class that were so boring they would give an aspirin a headache. Jesus avoided the "Bayer syndrome" by making His frequent lectures illustrated lectures. He sprinkled His lectures liberally with verbal and visual illustrations and object lessons.

Many of Christ's lectures were given out in the countryside or on the seashore. What a place to teach—I mean, there would be so many distractions. I can see it all now—farmers working in the fields, fishermen tugging at nets, birds flying over, flowers to pick and smell. Trees, grass, weeds, even the sky can draw attention away from the speaker.

Jesus not only overcame these distractions; He recruited every one of them for visual aids. What would *you* do if, while you were speaking on a serious subject, a small child broke away from its mother and came toddling across the front of your outdoor sanctuary on his way to pick a flame-colored tiger lily? Would you lose your concentration? Call for an usher? Give the kid's mother a dirty look?

Not Jesus. Can't you just see Him take the curly-haired, smiling child in His arms and make a point about the childish simplicity that is a prerequisite for getting into heaven? Can you hear Him as He admires, with the child, the lily in the kid's fist? Do you hear Him tell the people not to worry about what they will wear because a loving God who dresses up a meadow with lilies more beautiful than old Solomon's wardrobe, surely cares for them?

When the class members' eyes turned from the Speaker to a farmer planting a crop, Jesus didn't clear His throat and wait in ominous silence for the class to come to attention. He turned to look at the farmer with them and promptly hitched a ton of truth to the scene of the farmer sowing in the field. Jesus spoke of the judgment in terms of a weedy wheat field. The kingdom of heaven was compared to a tree that had grown from a tiny mustard seed, and to a fish net that drew in rough fish and edible.

After a long session of instruction on the night that Jesus was betrayed, the pruning of a vineyard became the "clincher" that drove home an unforgettable lesson. After the Last Supper, Jesus leads His disciples past the vineyards in the Kidron valley on their way to Gethsemane. Watch Jesus as He stands in the midnight moonlight and instructs His disciples. He picks up a dead twig from a smoldering fire left by the pruners. "I am the vine, you are the branches; he who abides in Me . . . bears much fruit . . . If anyone does not abide in Me, he is thrown away as a branch, and dries up; and they gather them, and cast them into the fire."[7] Can you hear the twig snap in His hand as He extends His arm slowly, holds it poised for a long second, and drops the broken branch into the fire? Can you sense the meaning in the heavy silence of the disciples as they watch? It was one illustrated lecture they never grew old enough to forget.

Earlier, on this eve of His execution, Jesus had had much to say to His followers. He wanted them to understand—really understand—the meaning of His sacrificial death. He lectured at length, then climaxed the session with the Lord's Supper. He showed them the bread and the wine—things they could see (and touch and smell and taste). This lesson entered their experience through all five senses. This makes a lesson last. Even today, nearly 2,000 years later, the five senses involved in this sacrament lift the level of our worship to the sublime.

We have talked a lot about Jesus' use of teaching aids. In one sense Jesus was himself a Teaching Aid. Ever since Adam and Eve ran to hide from Him, God has been seeking man. He revealed himself through the law and the prophets. When these served their purpose, He gave us Someone we could *see.* He sent His Son, emptied out in condescension, in the form of sinful flesh, so we could see and understand what God was like. As Arnold Prater has written, "On Calvary the God of all the galaxies . . . [is] shouting to us in crystal clear terms, 'I care. I love you. I love you this much.'"[8]

Chapter 9

Teaching for Transformation

*The Ultimate Goal of
Adult Christian Education*

Ruth Henck

When people learn, they change. To use familiar educational parlance, learning produces change in three areas: (1) what one knows (cognitive domain); (2) what one feels (affective domain), and (3) what one does (psychomotor domain).

Christian teachers of adults aim for change in each of these areas. We want our students to *know* more about the Bible, to *appreciate* the Christ-style life, and to respond *behaviorally,* applying Christian principles to life situations.

The mere threefold change sought by secular educators must not satisfy the Christian teacher. His or her job must go farther. A deeper dimension of change is the target of Christian educators—*the transformation of human lives by the power of God.*

RUTH HENCK is a member of the editorial staff of the Department of Church Schools, Church of the Nazarene Headquarters, Kansas City, Mo. She holds an A.B. degree from Olivet Nazarene College and an M.A. in education from the University of Missouri. She has taken graduate work in journalism at the University of Missouri and the University of Kansas.

The Christian teacher prays and plans to help his students become new creatures in Christ. "Therefore if any man be in Christ, he is a new creature: old things are passed away; behold, all things are become new" (2 Cor. 5: 17). Further, he seeks to help his students experience the sanctifying power of the Holy Spirit. "And God . . . bare them witness giving them the Holy Ghost . . . purifying their hearts by faith" (Acts 15:8-9). Beyond this, Christian teaching must assist persons in living the transformed life —"be not conformed to this world: but be ye transformed by the renewing of your mind, that ye may prove what is that good, and acceptable, and perfect, will of God" (Rom. 12:2). "The path of the just is as the shining light, that shineth more and more unto the perfect day" (Prov. 4:18).

Transforming Teaching

Teaching for transformation is not achieved by a casual concept of duty, or a halfhearted approach to the task. The following are some of the elements of transforming teaching.

Love Your Students. Every student who comes to your class must soon understand that he or she has a teacher who cares. A coldhearted teacher, even though he may possess fabulous knowledge or have a string of degrees, is almost useless. The Christian teacher must love his students and let them know it. He must be willing to get involved in their lives beyond the classroom as well as being sensitive to human need within the classroom.

When the early Christians met together in their house churches to pray, worship, and share, they found a divine dimension of fellowship which they called *koinonia*. In bearing one another's burdens, they found their own burdens borne. They made it as Christians in a hostile society because they loved and helped each other.

Koinonia is still in style, and it must happen in your class if transformation is to occur.

Present the Plan of Salvation. God's plan of salvation should be taught, clarified, and explained. No student should sit long in your class without hearing this. Your teaching of salvation should not only include clear Christian conversion but sound, straightforward instruction about entire sanctification. Some teachers let sanctification die of neglect, and consequently the transformation they hope for never comes to full harvest.

Make the Bible Your Textbook. Even when you begin your session by focusing upon a social problem or life situation, you must not fail to proceed to the biblical solution. Scripture knowledge must be initially developed so the student has certain awarenesses of the plan of salvation. He must be aware of the condition of man—"For all have sinned, and come short of the glory of God" (Rom. 3:23). He must be aware of the remedy for sin—"For God so loved the world, that he gave his only begotten Son, that whosoever believeth in him should not perish, but have everlasting life" (John 3:16). He must be aware of the condition and promise of God for forgiveness—"If we confess our sins, he is faithful and just to forgive us our sins, and to cleanse us from all unrighteousness" (1 John 1:9). And he must be aware of the approachability of God—"Him that cometh unto me I will in no wise cast out" (John 6:37).

At times when a person is ready, basic scripture knowledge can lead directly to a crisis transformation. Consider the case of "Don Smith."

Don was 25, single, and engrossed in a Ph.D. program in experimental psychology at a prestigious Midwestern university. Most of his days were spent in the laboratory, and he had very little time for socializing.

One Sunday morning he decided to get up early, meander downtown, and browse through the art gallery. To shorten the story, Don never got downtown. The sign in the front of a church near his apartment announced, "Singles Bible Class—Room 54." Don went. That morning the Holy Spirit spoke through the Word, and Don Smith found the Lord. Listen to his testimony:

"I never knew much about the Bible. Oh, we all said the Lord's Prayer in grade school. That was before the Supreme Court ruling. Anyhow, when I heard that Sunday school teacher say, 'We've all sinned,' I began to think. I guess I knew I was a sinner all along—I just never thought much about it. Then when a guy about my age told how he had found Christ, and when I read in the lesson book, 'But if we confess our sins, he is faithful and just to forgive us,' I knew what I had to do. That morning was the turning point in my life, and I've never regretted it. I'll always be thankful for that Sunday school class where God's Word was studied."

For a person to live a transformed life, scripture knowledge must increase. Bible-use skills must be developed. Exposure to Bible study in your class should help the student learn to use the Bible for himself as a Resource for learning appropriate modes of behavior and for gaining spiritual strength to live victoriously.

Pray a Lot. Another skill we need to teach is prayer. Initially, prayer skill must be developed to the point where the student knows how to ask God for forgiveness. This ability is most often gained simply by hearing someone else pray.

Later, the student must develop and maintain a vital prayer life. He must experience the delightful presence of God that comes as we draw near to Him in prayer. He must know how to offer prayers of praise, of thanksgiving, and of intercession. And he must know the value God places on prayer: "The effectual fervent prayer of a righteous man availeth much" (Jas. 5:16).

Prayer experiences in the Sunday school class often create in the student a deep appreciation for prayer and a desire to develop a meaningful prayer relationship.

Lead the Evangelized to Become Evangelists. To keep the ministry of transformation going, the Christian teacher of adults must help motivate and equip students to share their faith. At the time of His ascension, Christ's parting words were: "Ye shall be witnesses unto me both in Jerusalem, and in all Judaea, and in Samaria, and unto the uttermost part of the earth" (Acts 1:8).

Challenge Students with Stewardship. Do not be afraid to challenge your pupils to adopt a high standard of sacrificial stewardship. Stress the stewardship of money. Those who bypass this dimension in favor of other areas of stewardship are frequently trying to evade the issue. Every Christian should be a tither. Of course a full-orbed stewardship includes a sacramental regard for service, time, energy, health, and abilities as well as money. Keep the call to Christian service ringing in the ears and consciences of your class members.

Create a Climate for Change

If a climate for change is to exist, students must feel a sense of freedom to express personal ideas and attitudes without recrimination. They must feel a sense of personal worth, both to themselves and to others.

Next, students must come in contact with influences and conditions which tend to *cause* change. Some of the most effective influences are associations with another person or a group of persons, and the gaining of new knowledge, new feelings, or new skills. Some of the most effective conditions are feeling a need that must be met, experiencing conflict or stress, or setting a goal. All of these influences and conditions can be beautifully supplied when people meet together to study the Word of God.

Various before-class activities give adults opportunity to develop associations and relationships which may cause change. Often, just "being" with Christian people is enough to cause the unsaved to feel the need for God and to seek a personal relationship with Him. For the Christian, fellowship with other believers often moves one toward a deeper walk of faith and Christian commitment.

In some churches students meet 20-30 minutes early to report calls made on absentees, fill out cards for new class prospects, and outline the next week's visitation program. Other adult classes meet early to enjoy a continental breakfast together. In other cases, the time before class gives opportunity to implement creative group projects—such as practicing for a dramatic presentation, planning a panel discussion, or researching a group report. Activities such as these often provide a needed cohesiveness and a sense of comradeship that would otherwise be missing.

Teaching for transformation means that Sunday school lessons must be more than an interesting presentation of content material. Although content *is* important, we must also concentrate on teaching the skills of Christian living. We must equip our students with the spiritual skills needed to cope with the stresses and challenges of life. These skills then must be presented in a way which relates to the student, for learning occurs only within a context of meaning.

Thus the transformation mandate has something to say about the teaching methods we use. If the teacher is a nonstop lecturer, he never knows whether his students are progressing or regressing. He or she cannot take inventory (discover where his students are in regard to the subject matter), nor can he evaluate how much learning has occurred.

Teaching procedures which require student participation make it possible to take inventory, to evaluate attitudes and feelings, to test learning, and to guide the class properly. Role play is one of the best techniques for accomplishing these goals. Discussion, agree-disagree exercises, and content quizzes can be used to inventory and evaluate attitude change.

Bible-based involvement learning is not used merely for the teacher's inventory, however. Such activities are educationally sound. They reinforce learning, and in the interaction the student compares and adjusts his ideas, interpretations, and knowledge with that of his peers.

God's call to be a Christian teacher is a call to teach for transformation—to persuade your students in Christ's stead to answer the call to salvation and service with a "Here am I; send me."

No matter how brilliant our students think we are, no matter how many flattering accolades they heap upon us for our ingenuity, we must not be entirely satisfied with anything less than teaching that transforms.

Chapter 10

Grow and Go

A Training and Enrichment Program for Adult Teachers

Earl C. Wolf

Only when we believe that what we are doing for the Lord is of utmost importance will we accept the discipline our task demands. Our concept of the role of adult leadership is the dominant factor in the investment of our energies and resources in the teaching ministry God has given us.

In the early days of the New Testament Church, Jesus underscored the importance of leadership. He gave major attention in His ministry to the training of the Twelve.

EARL C. WOLF is the executive director of the Christian Service Training Commission for the Church of the Nazarene. He graduated from Eastern Nazarene College and has done graduate study at Evangelical and Reformed Theological Seminary, and Seattle Pacific College. In 1972 he was awarded the Doctor of Divinity degree by Eastern Nazarene College.

Dr. Wolf served as a pastor for 16 years. His many church assignments have included editor of adult Church Schools publications, Church of the Nazarene, for 17 years; and part-time instructor in religious education at Nazarene Theological Seminary. He is the author of several books, including *My Gold and My God, The Living Word,* and *Better Adult Teaching.* He also authored the "Proverbs" section of *Beacon Bible Commentary.*

Concerned about the growth and strengthening of the Church, He designated five significant ministries—that of apostles, prophets, evangelists, pastors, and teachers (Eph. 4:11). All these ministries were considered essential to the work of the Kingdom.

We value highly the first four ministries Jesus designated. But sometimes we fail to realize fully the significance of the fifth designation—the teaching ministry. It was no doubt rightly stated that a good Sunday school curriculum is 90 percent teacher and 10 percent materials. Surely it is helpful to have good literature, effective organization, and adequate facilities and equipment to aid us in our teaching task. But the primary factor in Christian teaching is the dedicated, Spirit-filled teacher. It was Marion Lawrence who said, "The greatest need in the church today is for trained teachers who will put the whole mind into preparation, the whole soul into presentation, and the whole life into illustration."

Many expressions have been used to describe the role of the teacher of adults. He is a "lead learner," or a "learning leader." He is a "playing coach," or a "facilitator of learning experiences." Whatever terminology one chooses to describe his work, the teacher is more than one who simply "dishes out information," even though it be biblical information. He is a spiritual leader.

As a religious leader, the teacher is aware of the importance of the quality of his own life. He is sensitive to the fact that "the teacher's life is the life of his teaching." He is eager to give attention to the cultivation of the Christian virtues. He wants the fruit of the Spirit to be evidenced in his life.

While his task is primarily spiritual, he does not minimize the importance of continuing education, of learning new teaching methods and skills. He does not look lightly upon the necessity of adequate lesson preparation. He does not discount the imperative of such matters as an understanding of the doctrine of holiness, the basic beliefs of the Christian faith, the Word of God, the history of his denomination, and the meaning of church membership. He does not reject those resources that will help him to be a faithful workman. He is mindful of Paul's counsel to Timothy that he be "sanctified . . . and prepared unto every good work" (2 Tim. 2:21).

The effective adult teacher has not arrived, but is arriving. He is not only a growing Christian but a growing teacher. He does not crush his laurels by resting on them. His diplomas, degrees, or certificates are not permitted to check his development. His past educational attainments are used to accomplish the Christian education objectives of his adult class, department, and church. He relates the work he is doing in the Sunday school to the total mission of the church. Even competent business and professional people need to understand the special nature of their task in the Sunday school. Teachers of varying educational backgrounds and accomplishments need to continue to learn and grow in order to be effective. The late Dr. Orval J. Nease said, "In the work of God, one must be more than good; he must be resourceful."

Training and Enrichment Opportunities

There are many training and enrichment opportunities today for teachers of adults. Some churches operate a regular training program. Such a program is unquestionably of value in developing an effective staff. But beyond a highly structured program there are many informal and flexible opportunities for the training and enrichment of adult teachers.

As there is no one *best* method for teaching adults, perhaps there is no one *best* method for training adult teachers. The full spread of training opportunities suggested here will not likely be available in any one church. But there are usually sufficient opportunities everywhere to challenge the resourceful teacher.

Teacher Training Programs. In order to give guidance to their Sunday school teachers, most denominations conduct some form of teacher training program. Every teacher who seeks to give his best to Christ and to the church will wish to continue to grow, and this will call for participation in such training programs. This will bring added competence and a sense of deep personal satisfaction.

Regular Workers' Meetings. These meetings are excellent opportunities for training. They are designed for the growth of the workers. They are not planned primarily for business but for inspiration, study, and discussion. In the sharing of ideas, much help is gained by officers, teachers, and prospective workers.

Home Study Courses. Many training courses are available by home study. This correspondence plan makes training available right in a teacher's living room or at his kitchen table. When a teacher cannot attend scheduled training classes, home study provides an answer and offers "training unlimited." Many times courses of a specialized nature cannot be offered in local church classes. The home study plan puts training within the reach of all teachers regardless of the size of their church.

Cooperative Training Schools. Often teachers can continue their training by attending a zone, city-wide, or district training school. Many times a local church is unable to offer the variety of courses that such a school or institute can. A cooperative school often affords a greater spread of resource people.

In-service Training. In many churches the leadership shortage is so acute that nearly all the emerging or potential leaders have already been put in places of responsibility. Often these leaders feel inadequate for the assignments. But on a learn-as-you-go basis they gain confidence and equip themselves for the work God has for them to do. In-service training is, of course, not only for the newer worker but for the more experienced leader as well.

Growth Through Reading. A number of denominations have set up guided reading courses for teachers and workers. This plan encourages each worker to read articles in teachers' magazines and Christian education quarterlies, as well as full-length books. It also recommends listening to instructional tapes and cassettes.

Visits to Other Churches or Schools. Teachers need models. Often they are enriched by watching others at work. When on vacation, they can observe other teachers in their class settings. Once or twice a year they may want to turn their classes over to assistants and visit other churches to see how others do their job. They can pick up helpful ideas that will improve the work they are doing with their own classes.

Cadet or Apprenticeship Teaching. New teachers gain valuable help by observing and assisting experienced teachers. After some months of this association, the new teacher may be ready to accept a class of his own.

Conventions and Workshops. Many teachers have the opportunity to attend Sunday school conventions where there are resources and instruction available. These occasions provide much help for the local worker. Often specific workshops are held in connection with conventions. These workshops are especially helpful to those who are eager to improve. Sometimes workshops are held at district centers or on college campuses.

Improving Through Supervision. It is difficult for us to be objective about our own teaching. Our weaknesses are seldom as apparent to us as they are to others. It is, therefore, helpful to have the counsel of a pastor, Sunday school superintendent, our department supervisor, or the director of Christian education. Such a plan always requires an eagerness on the part of the new teacher to be helped. For this approach to be most helpful, a proper understanding of the role of supervisor is needed on the part of the person supervising.

Supply Teaching. Every department of the Sunday school should have a group of reserve teachers. Their teaching, however, would not be as frequent as that of the cadet or apprentice teacher. Supply teachers can work with classes when the regular teacher may be absent. They can teach occasionally with the regular teacher present. In either case they are getting valuable experience for use in future assignments.

Self-improvement Guide. A number of denominations have developed teacher's self-improvement guides. These instruments are designed to help a person analyze his teaching practices and evaluate himself as a teacher. It is well periodically for a teacher to check himself against such a yardstick.

Library Resources. Church or public libraries offer a wide range of resources for the teacher. Sometimes the library of a local or nearby educational institution offers much help. Too often adults have thought of these resources as belonging to their "school days," not realizing that they continue to offer them help as long as they are eager to learn.

Local College or Continuing Education Programs. A training resource that should not be overlooked by adult teachers is that of the local college. Here courses such as speech, psychology or interpersonal relationships, and education or educational media could be highly rewarding. A number of colleges and universities offer Continuing Education courses, with both credit and non-credit courses available. Many communities have adult education courses that would be of value to the teacher. More and more adults are availing themselves of these resources for the purpose of improving their skills and professions. By doing so, they improve their chances for increased earnings. If people in the secular world can continue their education for that purpose, Christian teachers should continue their training to serve the Lord in a more acceptable way.

Tape and Audiovisual Resources. A wide variety of audio materials are available for personal enrichment today. Often cassettes provide enrichment for a teacher's devotional life, guidance in Bible study, and help in learning new teaching techniques. Many audiovisuals—both films and filmstrips—bring similar help to the teacher. This type of resource can be found in the church or local library. Some churches have established an Audiovisual Resource Center, where both tapes and films are cataloged. More teachers than ever before are finding help from these media.

A Basic Library for Bible Study

It is difficult to think of a training and enrichment program for adult teachers without considering some basic tools to help them better understand and teach the Word of God. In addition to the curriculum materials provided by his denomination, the resourceful leader is looking for those tools which will enable him to be a better workman with the Word.

A Good Study Bible. A valuable aid for the teacher today is a good study Bible. Such a tool is helpful in tracing the various references on a particular theme. For example, the *Thompson Chain-Reference Bible* has an excellent reference system, linking together the tens of thousands of Bible verses. The teacher will likely wish to examine a number of study Bibles and select the one best fitted to his needs. By writing his publishing house, the teacher may secure information on a complete line of reference Bibles.

An Exhaustive Concordance. Many Bibles have a limited concordance in the back. An exhaustive concordance, however, that lists each occurrence of every word in the Bible is an essential for diligent Bible study. Any reference can be located by recalling one significant word in the desired passage and looking up that word in the concordance. *Cruden's Complete Concordance* is the best-known concordance on the English Bible (King James Version). *Strong's Exhaustive Concordance* and *Young's Analytical Concordance* trace each word in the English text back to its Greek or Hebrew original. These concordances are leading resources for laymen.

A Bible Dictionary or Encyclopedia. These reference tools contain a wealth of information about people, places, customs, and things in the Bible. They contain drawings, illustrations, charts, and diagrams useful in our efforts to understand the Bible. Among the best Bible dictionaries in the field are: *Davis Dictionary of the Bible, The New Bible Dictionary,* and the *Zondervan Pictorial Bible Dictionary. The International Standard Bible Encyclopedia,* a five-volume set, is an older work, but a complete, conservative work of value.

Modern English Translations. The Bible student today has many modern English translations of the Bible or New

Testament to aid him in his study. No one of them can satisfy us equally well at every point. Every translation has its weaknesses as well as its strengths. Perhaps a viable approach to the use of these valuable resources would be to have two or three versions of the Bible and a similar number of paraphrases.

Among the most familiar versions are:
- King James Version
- *Revised Standard Version*
- *The New English Bible*
- *New American Standard Bible*
- *The Holy Bible—The Berkeley Version in Modern English*
- *The New International Version*

The most familiar paraphrases include:
- *The New Testament in Modern English,* by J. B. Phillips
- *Today's English Version (Good News for Modern Man)*
- *The Living Bible,* by Kenneth Taylor
- *The Amplified Bible*

A Bible Handbook. Perhaps the first background book a teacher should purchase is a good Bible handbook. Bible handbooks are packed full of information of all kinds for the Bible student. The most familiar books in this category are *Halley's Bible Handbook* and Donald E. Demaray's *Bible Study Sourcebook*.

Survey Volumes. To try to put together the whole picture of God's Revelation to us, we might turn to such survey volumes as *Exploring the Old Testament,* edited by W. T. Purkiser, and *Exploring the New Testament,* edited by Ralph Earle. Less extensive but helpful surveys are: *Know Your Old Testament,* by W. T. Purkiser, and *Know Your New Testament,* by Ralph Earle.

A Reliable Bible Atlas. A study Bible or Bible dictionary will usually contain maps of value to the teacher. These resources help the teacher to understand the historical and geographical setting of the Scriptures. Often a teacher desires added help, however, and this can be found in a reliable Bible atlas. Among the most useful are: *Baker's Bible Atlas, The Zondervan Pictorial Bible Atlas,* and *The Wycliffe Historical Geography of Bible Lands.*

A One-Volume Commentary. The one-volume commentary is less expensive than a multivolume set. It is a good place for the teacher to begin. Some will want to own the larger sets, of course. But among the one-volume, conservative commentaries are: *The New Bible Commentary: Revised, The Wycliffe Bible Commentary, Matthew Henry's Commentary* (edited by Leslie F. Church), and *Adam Clarke's Commentary* (abridged by Ralph Earle).

Beyond these basic tools for Bible study there are limitless resources. There are extensive Bible study helps available, such as the annual Sunday school commentaries, multivolume commentaries, and in-depth studies on single books. There are word and topical studies. There are also Bible histories and archaeological studies. Books on Bible manners and customs are also available.

A do-it-yourself working file is, of course, within the reach of every teacher—even those of very limited means. A file where the teacher can put newspaper clippings, pictures, quotes, and other materials from his reading that would relate the Bible to the needs of his class is a most usable resource. It is too often overlooked.

A Good Workman

Let us be mindful always that the teaching ministry is more than an assignment by the church school board or educational committee. It is a task that God has given us.

Paul's counsel to Timothy is appropriate: "Be a good workman, one who does not need to be ashamed when God examines your work. Know what his Word says and means" (2 Tim. 2:15, TLB).

Chapter 11

Organizing for Nurture and Outreach

Meaningful Activities in the Adult Class

Tom Barnard

Picture someone going up to Jesus during a break and saying, "Lord, we have this group of believers who meet each first-day morning in Capernaum. They wanted me to ask You if You had any good ideas for meaningful activities to help them fulfill their mission as one of Your groups."

Peter would probably reply before the Lord had a chance, "Don't you see that the Lord has more important things to do and say than to answer a question like that?"

TOM BARNARD is dean of student affairs and professor of religious education at Bethany Nazarene College. He holds degrees from Pasadena College (A.B.), Fuller Theological Seminary (M.R.E.), Bethany Nazarene College (M.A.), and Oklahoma State University (Ed.D.). Prior to his accepting a teaching position at Bethany Nazarene College, Dr. Barnard served in ministries of music, Christian education, youth, and as associate pastor in California. Dr. Barnard is president of the Oklahoma Sunday School Association. His articles have appeared in several Christian magazines, and he is the author of a book, *The Adult Class in Action*. A member of Bethany First Church of the Nazarene, Dr. Barnard teaches one of the largest adult classes in the denomination.

But just then, the Lord, in His characteristic way, would probably say, "Wait. Let's talk about that. I *am* interested in what My people do to multiply My ministry." So start with Jesus. If one can understand His mission, then one can understand better the mission of individuals and groups who follow His teachings.

Jesus had much to get done in a short period of time. Middle age for Him was 17. His active ministry was, at most, only three and a half years. Yet He was incredibly wise, and He established by His example and through His teachings a way of living which is as contemporary today as it was then. He saw that discipleship demanded personal involvement—giving, doing, going, dying. Total personal mobilization. And He generalized the standard for anybody who would take His name: "If any man would come after me, let him deny himself, and take up his cross, and follow me." Total *personal* mobilization: talent, time, treasure—then and now.

Likewise, groups of Christian adults today face corporately what the individual Christian faced then. The Great Commission is not diluted merely because a committee assumes responsibility for it. An adult Sunday school class mission is a macrocosm of the individual Christian's mission. It is total class mobilization for Christ.

The only problem is that some adult Christians act as if the Great Commission were a private, personal thing between a Christian and his Lord, subject only to divine accountability—and that at the Judgment. When they are asked to get involved in something more time-consuming than a class discussion, their excuses are legion. "I would love to, but . . ." However, Jesus' haunting words echo from the past: "I was hungry, and you fed me not. I was naked, and you clothed me not. I was in prison, and you visited me not . . . [therefore] I am none of yours." The question is not "Are we obligated as a class to get involved?" but "How can we best be used of God to fulfill the mission He has given to us through Jesus?"

Typically, that mission can best be understood as it is divided into three basic types of activities in the adult Sunday school class: serving activities, shepherding activities, and saving activities.

Serving Activities

Serving and being of service is no low-priority option for the Christian adult. Service is dead-center in the Christian ethic. The Lord said of himself, "The Son of Man came not to be ministered unto, but to minister" (Matt. 20:26). Concerning His closest friends, He said, "Whoever will be chief among you, let him be your servant" (Matt. 20:27). The Apostle John wrote: "We know what real love is from Christ's example in dying for us. And so we also ought to lay down our lives for our Christian brothers" (1 John 3:16, TLB).

One of the singles classes in the Sunday school was planning a weekend class retreat. Several of the mothers in the class had been divorced and lived on small incomes. They could not afford both the cost of the retreat and the cost of baby-sitting for their children while they were gone. The teacher of the singles class approached the teacher of a middle-age adult class in the Sunday school and asked if she could make an appeal for free baby-sitting for the mothers who wished to enjoy the retreat. The response to her appeal was spontaneous. The five mothers were freed from the worry of caring for their children for a weekend, and members of an adult class received a great blessing in being able to minister to someone else's needs.

Service projects can be as large-scale or as small-scale as an adult class is willing to accept for itself. The common ingredient is a need which no other group is adequately meeting. Service projects should be designed to follow simple principles.

1. They should be able to be completed within a relatively short period of time. Service projects that drag on for several weeks or months lose their appeal, and the interest of the class lags.

2. Service projects should be coordinated by someone (or some committee in the class) so that not more than one or two projects are being carried out at any one time.

3. Opportunity should be given to all members of the class to get involved in some activity throughout the year.

4. Persons who have participated in activities of this nature should receive public recognition and thanks for their effort.

5. Service projects should be done in such a way as to not embarrass the recipients.

6. Service projects should never be done with a desire to receive something (or some service or favor) in return for the service. The blessings received by the participating members of the class always far outweigh any reciprocal favor.

Only imagination and human resources limit the extent to which a class can be of service to others in need. One large adult class, with many talented members, put on a Christmas program for the entire church as its "Christmas present to the church." Music, drama, laughs, tears. An unforgettable evening during the Advent season. Another class established work parties, with class members going to homes of shut-ins and others, inviting men and women with handyman skills to join them in neighborly goodwill—repairing, painting, mowing, building. Another class took on the project of supplying Christmas gifts for all the children of an orphanage in another county. Ages, sex, and sizes of the children were supplied by the orphanage director. Class members "adopted" the children as their own and bought gifts for them. Delivering the gifts to the location was a celebration in itself.

Other service projects could include: (1) Sponsoring a Home Department Sunday for the church; (2) Providing a tutoring service for children in the community; (3) Reading for the blind, or delivering and playing cassette tapes of scriptures or the Sunday services to blind or shut-in members of the community; (4) Promoting a "Special Olympics" for handicapped or retarded children; (5) Providing the leadership for starting home Bible studies in the community.

Shepherding Activities

Shepherding activities are those which build a sense of community in the adult class and that meet social needs. Needing each other is not new. Meeting the needs of others in fellowship is not new, either. Among the last words spoken to Peter by the risen Saviour were words of a shepherding commitment. "Do you love me? . . . Feed my sheep."

Shepherding involves developing a sensitivity to others and responding as Christ would respond. Shepherding is not evangelizing. It is the activity of caring for the fellowship needs of those already evangelized. As opposed to "outreach" activities, shepherding activities are "inward" activities—the class "looking after its own." Few expressions of compliment from New Testament times were stronger than those spoken of the believers by those not of the fellowship: "Behold, how they love one another."

One adult class has an organized Retreat Scholarship Fund. Each year the class has its own retreat, with outside guest speaker and all. The class goes to a first-class lodge and eats well. The cost would be prohibitive for many in the class if it weren't for the scholarship fund. Each Sunday of the year, class members set aside an offering especially for the retreat. The frequent mention of it not only creates interest in going but also assures a generous fund by retreat time. Most of the retreat expenses are met in this way, including housing and meals. Couples who can well afford to pay for the entire cost for themselves often do so, leaving a balance to cover the costs for new couples, prospects, and special guests. The retreat has drawn over 50 in attendance each year since it was begun six years ago.

Another class builds "community" into its fellowship with a class "cooperative." This co-op meets monthly to purchase (at wholesale) foodstuffs for its own members. On a given Saturday the class members assemble to sack their own share. Not only are significant savings generated by the young couples, but their quality of caring fellowship is significantly improved.

The Career Class of one of Denver's large churches decided to stimulate laughter within its own group by staging a production featuring members performing in areas of complete inability! They called it the "Untalent Show." The number of persons participating was a surprise to all.

Shepherding activities cover many types of involvement. Class newsletters, various types of small-group fellowships, home Bible study groups during the week, study breakfasts or coffees, friendship visitation, parties, and backyard socials are examples of the kinds of fellowship class members frequently enjoy. One large adult class decided that its members did not know one another well enough. It started a special VIP portion of class each Sunday. One or two couples were interviewed by the class president during the class session. Their special interests, occupations, children, and hobbies were revealed. Class interest during those months of special introductions was unusually high.

Many adult classes conduct a presession fellowship at the class location, with coffee, juice, and sweet rolls served.

A committee elected each year by the class arranges for coffee, and class couples volunteer periodically by signing up for the rolls. Adults who can enjoy eating together have less difficulty sharing together in class discussion later.

Introduction of guests and visitors to the adult class can be a fruitful time of fellowship, if handled with care. Strangers generally do not enjoy being made to do anything which would draw undue attention to themselves. But they do enjoy being welcomed by a class greeter, introduced (but not asked to stand) by the class president, publicly greeted by the teacher, and surrounded by friendly class members after class. People who are treated in this manner will come back.

The world does not understand the kind of fellowship that Christians enjoy. It is one of those things which the world has not been able to package, market, or sell on television. We should do it better than anyone else.

Saving Activities

Saving activities are class efforts to evangelize the community. The commission to make disciples of all nations was spoken to Christians on the move—"going" saints. While it is true that many people will be won to Christ through the winsomeness of the fellowship of Christians who demonstrate their caring spirit in shepherding their own, evangelism bears most of its fruit through planned activities of outreach. Simply, outreach means evangelizing people for Christ. Of all the church auxiliaries, the Sunday school class is the one organization best suited for outreach roles.

1. It is a lay organization, involving lay persons in becoming equipped for their work of ministering.

2. The Sunday school class is committed to an educational ministry, offering organized programs for people to

study God's Word and to place people in direct confrontation with the claims of Christ for their lives.

3. The Sunday school is the one organization in the church where the unsaved are welcome as members! They can become involved before making a life commitment (which usually follows).

4. If adult classes are maintained at a modest size, and new ones started as needed, there is increased opportunity for growth in the Christian life as new Christians engage in close fellowship with other, more mature Christians.

5. Some of the best prospects for evangelism come from the adult class roll. Casual attenders and fringe families provide a class with a natural prospect list. "Deadwood" class members are some of the finest prospects a class can find. Showering them with sincere, consistent attention may bring them to a point of contact for sharing the good news of Jesus Christ.

An area of great need in metropolitan centers is the single parent. One out of every 10 children in the United States lives with a single parent. Of this number, 11 out of every 12 children who live with a single parent live with their mothers. When a family unit is broken, for any reason, many difficult adjustments must be made. Spiritual needs are intense among parents left to raise their children alone. The adult class has a unique opportunity to communicate Christ to all who need to meet Him.

There are at least two reasons why so many adult classes are not mobilized in their witnessing and soul-winning responsibilities: (1) they take the attitude that personal evangelism is "somebody else's job," and (2) they are not given tools to do the job well.

Principles of Soul Winning. At least six principles must be understood in order for effective evangelism to be operative within a Sunday school class.

1. It must be understood that soul winning is God's work. But it is work that He delegates. He will not do it alone; He needs a witness.

2. Soul winning begins with an example—a human example. Few people will be impressed with a Christian's witness if the Person witnessed about hasn't made a noticeable change in the Christian.

3. Soul winning begins where the people are. The "whitened harvest field" is where people are—where they live, work, relax. It is there where they are the most comfortable and the most uncomfortable. Because of their circumstances, they know that they have something lacking. Christ may be the One who can fill that void.

4. Soul winning should be the natural result of a person being confronted with a simple truth: "God loves you and has a special plan for your life."

5. Soul winning is based on the authority of God's Word, softened by God's love. Guilt is met with grace.

6. Soul winning requires a listening ear. Asking questions will encourage a prospect to share his feelings, to ascertain his background, to stimulate his own thinking and imagination, to concentrate on his problems and needs, and to allow God to speak to his situation.

7. Soul winning requires training. Helter-skelter evangelism often leads to helter-skelter Christians.

Bud Wilkinson, famed former coach of the Oklahoma University football Sooners, was asked during a speech in Dallas to describe football as a game. "The game of football," he replied, "may be described as a game in which there are 22 men on the field who desperately need rest and about 40,000 people in the stands who desperately need exercise." While the numbers may not apply to an adult

Sunday school class, the principle of involvement is relevant. The commission of Jesus Christ asks that the spectators leave the stands and get involved in what's going on down on the field of play. The adult class provides the opportunity. It has the means to get more people "into the game."

Chapter 12

Seen and Noted

*An Adventure in
Adult Christian Education*

Waulea Renegar

"The trouble with Christianity, Waulea, is it just doesn't work in the home."

This reply to an invitation to attend my Sunday school class left me stammering. The young business executive spoke without any irritation. He simply stated his reason for not investing his Sunday mornings in church classes. The impact of his statement was the more jarring because his wife and children had been regular attenders of our church for some time. In fact, his wife had been a Christian for over 10 years, and his evaluation of Christianity's contribution to their home was chilling.

WAULEA RENEGAR graduated from Washburn University and has attended several other colleges and universities. She has earned a number of honors, including being elected to Outstanding Young Women of America. She was named Sunday School Teacher of the Year for the Southern California District, Church of the Nazarene.

She is a popular retreat and convention speaker for various religious groups. She has served as supervising teacher of Los Angeles and Orange counties, Calif., for the Andelin Foundation for Education in Family Living. She is married to Rev. Wallace R. Renegar and is the mother of a son and daughter.

This encounter made a lasting impression upon my approach to Sunday school teaching. I no longer teach lessons, I teach students.

My teaching changes did not come quickly nor without confusing alterations. I did not know exactly where to begin, but I knew the first step had to be a way of determining where my class was spiritually.

As I began looking for ideas to measure spiritual maturity, I found few resources. What I wanted was a sort of Christianity Achievement Test which measured what a student knew and applied to his daily life. I found no such test, but I did come across helpful teaching techniques.

One such technique was the usually helpful group work method. This teaching tool involves dividing students into small groups and giving them questions which they are to answer from the resources of the individuals. The following Sunday morning I fed what I considered leading questions to the students and instructed them to arrive at useful answers within 15 minutes. Each group was to select a spokesman who would report the findings when we reassembled for the concluding 15 minutes.

1. What is the hardest thing for you to do as a Christian?
2. What is an ideal Christian?
3. How should being a Christian affect your home?

The groups selected spokesmen. They talked. I announced the two-minute wrap-up warning. They noted my warning and talked until I called, "Time is up." Dutifully they turned their chairs back into the class setting. They smiled at me. I smiled at them.

"Group One, what is the hardest thing for you to do as a Christian?"

Group One answered, "Praying."

I waited. The spokesman looked at me pleasantly. I

prompted, "And . . ." She added, trying to please me, "And how hard it is to do."

"Group Two," I asked next. I was smiling, but my confidence was shaken. How could people talk for 15 minutes and end up with eight words?

"We think an ideal Christian is someone who is truly Christlike. They are Christlike in everything they do."

Group Three, answering the question how should being a Christian affect your home, replied, "It should really affect everything in your home."

I quickly learned that a teaching technique is no more effective than the preparation preceding it. I had thought up three questions. They thought up three answers.

I might not have known what to try next if it had not been for a bright young student who loved to debate controversial topics. He leveled a pertinent question at me. It was loaded and meant to stir up emotions, but it was a question I had wondered about myself.

My usual reaction to such questions was to referee the ensuing argument. I would jump in wherever I could, but I often added no more than the disturbed students—personal opinions. There were few knowledgeable exchanges because the questions occurred spontaneously and were answered spontaneously. On some occasions I actually taught the prepared lessons, but the aliveness was missing which the verbal exchange had fostered. I can remember secretly resigning every Sunday afternoon for the first six months I taught those alert, energetic adults.

It was on a Sunday with my lesson well prepared and point two underway that this bright nonbeliever threw out one of his provoking questions. I had had a good night's sleep and probably a good breakfast, because I found myself amused and answered: "You ask the most difficult questions." Then I looked at him squarely and asked, "Do you know what I'm going to do this week?" His expression altered slightly. "I'm going to find an answer to that question."

There were a few absentees the following Sunday, but Mr. Bright was not one of them. I had an answer lifted from some superficial study I had made from my home resources, and I felt pleased with my answer. He shot it full of holes. The class responded negatively to him. I was thinking that since I had tried to answer his question, he should have been satisfied. The quality of the answer was not the issue. The teacher had tried and that was sufficient. He was exhilarated. I felt exposed. Listening to my inadequate, shallow teaching being debated was both unsettling and painful.

Getting Down to the Real Issue

For some months I had been a member of a small prayer group which met weekly. Being personally deflated and utterly confused, I made myself vulnerable to these devout women. I confessed my inadequacy and revealed the class's obvious disinterest in spiritual matters. "They really come alive when God and the church are losing the argument," I explained tearfully. "Jesus is really optional to them."

We began to pray. The Holy Spirit led our praying and opened my understanding. My past lessons had been missing more than the bull's-eye; they were missing the entire target. I had been teaching on stewardship, discipline, and Christian heritage. But my class was made up of unbelievers and a few wavering church members. I received this important insight at the prayer session. Many were to follow as the prayer group became an important part of each new method I applied.

I had my starting point—unbelief. I was to begin teaching material they needed to know in order to believe in Jesus Christ. I set out on my first clue: Mr. Bright's original question. The remaining days of that week I did what I initially said I would. I sought an answer. I have rarely read more nor researched more diligently for a term paper than I dug for that answer. I came up with material so helpful to me personally I could not wait to share it. That feeling remains to this day in my classroom presentations.

On Sunday the young man followed me outside at the conclusion of class. "You are the first teacher who ever took my questions seriously," he said. In his eyes I read his real struggling need. My heart was spangled with joy.

In subsequent class sessions others ventured questions they had before felt disloyal to verbalize or had felt would raise eyebrows. Some asked questions which had been personally perplexing and defeating. Many probed with statements their unsaved friends had made to them. I felt as if I had a tiger by the tail and couldn't let go. There seemed to be no place to turn loose and return to my former safety.

As surely as the Holy Spirit teaches us about daily living, He teaches teachers how to teach. I had up to this point been depending heavily upon my natural ability to instruct and upon what special training I had had, and these had become a snare. The Spirit was desiring to make something unique of me as a teacher. He had further plans to make my class unique.

Daring weekly to probe for answers and then assemble those into teachable outlines, I began to observe the aura of belief settling about us. The drowsy believers were rousing. Unbelievers were developing hunger pains. I thrilled to see the Holy Spirit at work.

A Little Vision Helps a Lot

A new insight was readying itself. I attended a workshop and heard the challenge to visualize what you want God to do for you and enjoy it by faith until it becomes fact. I was ripe for such daring; and when blank sheets of paper were passed to each listener, I wrote boldly: "I am enjoying teaching a class of 50." At home I clipped this vision onto my Sunday school roll which at the time recorded an average attendance of only 15.

Sunday morning I confided my vision to the class. "Something remarkable is going to happen this year. I want to announce it now in order that we may praise God for it when it arrives." There was no stir of enthusiasm. I should not have expected any. It was my vision, not theirs.

The next step was clear. I called a meeting of the born-again class members. I shared my vision and asked them to accept it as theirs. Teachers do not produce great classes any more than shepherds produce great flocks of sheep. Teachers lead and instruct students, but students reproduce themselves. As their needs are met, they bring others to experience the same satisfaction. My position was to instruct. Theirs was to reproduce. Excitement charged the circle of 10.

In succeeding Sundays I sounded for depth. I devised questionnaires which uncovered spiritual weaknesses. Immediately common ones rose like cream on milk. How do you serve other people? It was one thing to commit oneself to a vision. It was another matter to become a part of it.

How do you serve a sinner when he asks you for help? What do you do when a disgruntled backslider softens under your witness and inquires, "How do I find my way back?" How do you respond when a highly moral person matches his standards against yours and sees little difference? Which approach do you make when antagonistic people attack the church, yet hold onto your friendship with strained need?

The steps forward were coming more easily. Obviously, these questions needed answers; and who better to answer them than an expert? I polled the class for special-interest types with whom most of the class associated. The 10 types tallied were moral nonbelievers, intellectuals, unsanctified believers, antagonistic nonbelievers, addicts and alcoholics, single adults, parolees, struggling newborns, lukewarm church members, and next-door neighbors.

Locating the experts was surprisingly easy. I found several within the class and the remainder within the church. I merely approached individuals who had been members of each of these 10 types and had come through unbelief into belief, from defeat into victory. Who better to ask about how to approach a disgruntled backslider than a backslider who had found his way home? How did he do it? Who helped him?

I allowed one month for each expert to prepare a 20-minute presentation, requiring that they all present a written outline in order that we might reproduce their findings in booklet form as a reference. During their month of preparation and prayer, I taught elective lessons on genuine Christianity, Christ's standards for believers as opposed to the world's standard, the dignity of serving, and motivation in service with its pitfalls of personal dishonesty, self-elevation, personal therapy, and servile duty.

This insight had come without seeking it. It was that teaching should be a reciprocal experience. The Holy Spirit teaches all: students and teachers. It was time for the teacher to be taught by the students. The Holy Spirit wisely instructed me not to mentally rephrase the students' comments in order to clarify their findings in my own words. I enjoyed their insights and profited from them with approving, but silent, lips. It is important for a teacher to accept the fact that clarity of truth is not his or her personal possession.

The unit was an unqualified success. Within months the class attendance began to rise. New people were coming. Old prospects were returning. Sporadic attenders were becoming regular. The vision was becoming sight. The 50 was an actuality, and accompanying the numbers came the miracle of new births—41 of them as the tally now shows. Not only did the class grow, the church did as well. In one year more than 60 members joined the church as a result of the ministry of the Koinonia Class.

In five years I have watched this Koinonia Class affect the spiritual well-being of the entire congregation. At this writing there are 23 teachers and supervisors who were members of this class and now serve in other areas of our church. Nine church board members have been elected from its roll, and the NYPS president, church choir director, church organist, vacation Bible school director, Children of Light musical group, and Caravan director are members. Five ministers are alumni, with four of the five settling their call during their days of class attendance. The Koinonia Class has grown in wisdom and stature from quarreling children to robust, mature adults redemptively touching lives in every area of the church.

Notes and Observations

No two classes are ever the same. Like individuals, a class has personality and character; and as these grow, needs change. I watched new light and genuine obedience alter the class. I had to commit myself to keeping up with them and determining where they were spiritually. I used resources from the Unified Sunday School Lessons, Dialog Series, Christian Service Training books, commentaries, religious and educational literature, and books on subjects I had never before considered a part of the Sunday school curriculum. I knew if the class had a need, God had the answer. I looked until His source was revealed and then confidently shared it. I admit this is time-consuming, but not endless. God is more interested in the students' needs than you are as a teacher. He will help you.

I learned how to prepare questionnaires which the students took periodically to expose areas of weakness and misinformation and reveal points of strength and knowledge. Sample questionnaires are found in many educational books, and these can be used as patterns in preparing spiritual ones. I have found questionnaires most valuable in determining the current spiritual position of the class.

I have observed that class success should not depend upon the omnipresence of the teacher. Student leadership should form the foundation of the class. Train officers and project chairmen to report to their elected president, not the teacher. The president should call all meetings and preside over them. My pastor was helpful in this matter, for I had never trained leaders. His instructions on organization and training ideas have helped me have time to prepare the lessons. The class's strength must belong to the students, much as the church's strength belongs to its members. A creative president is essential.

Flexible class procedures were another discovery. Class time should belong to the students. Innovations will come as needs change. Sharing time became important to the Koinonia Class. It was a segment used for sharing victories, telling incidents in which the lesson had been applied, or acknowledging personal need or defeat. The latter were immediately taken to prayer. Sharing time was productive because any truth is best sold by a satisfied consumer.

One student remarked, "I need a teacher who is filled with the love of Jesus, excited about being a Christian, patient and understanding, willing to listen and able to keep confidences, sincere and challenging, and (if possible after all that) still human enough that I can relate to her."

I have found that relating is in direct ratio with a teacher's willingness to expose her humanity to her students. Admit your failures and weaknesses. Better still, use them as illustrations which your students can use as "how-not-tos." There is a precious boldness which comes when you are vulnerable to students. You can approach them with the most pointed personal questions about their spiritual condition and have honest exchanges. I have led several students to the Lord with straight talk. Those who are loved always know it, and love is granted liberties.

Further, I have observed that the balance of believers must outnumber the nonbelievers. Belief and love are felt emotionally, just as unbelief and disinterest are. Request that your Sunday school superintendent work with you by not removing more students from your class than you can spiritually afford. If you maintain the aura of belief, believers will produce themselves, and he will then have a continuing field from which to harvest teachers.

Believe in the class. Never become defensive. Do not set yourself apart from them. Believe they want to learn. Do not talk about what absentees are not doing. Teach, praise, love, and concentrate upon the students who are there. Students tend to become what you think they are.

Pray specifically for individual students rather than the growth of the class. Talk to Jesus about their weaknesses, but thank Him for their strengths. Believe He hears you. Visualize that nonbeliever saved and living for Jesus. Picture that disinterested member as wide-awake and in love with God. Expect God to do the unusual. Carry His answer in your hand as confidently as you carry His Word. Jesus only gives what you know He has resources to supply.

Plan regular social events. Class members who do not

know each other socially are not as open nor as honest in class discussion. There is no substitute for your class knowing you on a social level as well as in the classroom situation.

A New Quality of Life

Before the preparation of this chapter, I interviewed this remarkable class, asking, "What change do you recognize in your life that is a direct result of this class?" A few were revealing:

"I am now able to become involved with others in a way never before possible. I can show love and concern for others without the fear of being hurt. My feeling of self-worth has increased, and I am less self-conscious and more at peace with myself and others."

"I am now able to see the things I have done wrong and correct them. I am more calm with my children, and I am slowly improving my faults in the relationship with my husband."

"I can directly attribute my salvation to the class. The lessons on God's love brought me back from a backslidden condition."

"I'm not so hard on myself as I used to be."

"The most important, above all else, is that I have become a born-again, Spirit-filled Christian because of this class."

The young executive who had commented, "The trouble with Christianity, Waulea, is that it just doesn't work in the home," made one of the foregoing statements. Praise the Lord!

Reference Notes

CHAPTER 1:

1. Earl F. Zeigler, *Christian Education of Adults* (Philadelphia: The Westminster Press, 1958), p. 31.
2. Roy B. Zuck and Gene A. Getz, eds., *Adult Education in the Church* (Chicago: Moody Press, 1970), p. 10.
3. Jerold W. Apps, *How to Improve Adult Education in Your Church* (Minneapolis, Minn.: Augsburg Publishing House, 1972), p. 74.
4. Paul Bergevin, *A Philosophy for Adult Education* (New York: The Seabury Press, 1967), p. 8.
5. James Williams, *Guiding Adults* (Nashville: Convention Press, 1969), p. 7.
6. Lyle Schaller, *The Change Agent* (Nashville: Abingdon Press, 1972), pp. 137-38. (Schaller quotes Steve Allen at this point.)
7. Bergevin, *Philosophy,* p. 5.
8. Apps, *Adult Education,* p. 99.
9. Paul Johnson, *Psychology of Religion* (New York: Abingdon Press, 1959), p. 285.
10. Vance Packard, *The Hidden Persuaders* (New York: David McKay Co., Inc., 1957), p. 3.
11. Reuel Howe, *The Miracle of Dialogue* (Greenwich: The Seabury Press, 1963), pp. 136-41.
12. John Drakeford, *The Awesome Power of the Listening Ear* (Waco, Tex.: Word Books, 1967), p. 15.
13. *Ibid.,* p. 44.
14. *Ibid.,* p. 48.
15. *Ibid.,* p. 63.

CHAPTER 2:

1. Allen J. Moore, *The Young Adult Generation* (Nashville and New York: Abingdon Press), pp. 16-17.
2. *Ibid.,* pp. 42, 44.

3. *Ibid.*, p. 80.

4. Vernon C. Grounds, "The Revolt Against Rationalism," in *Christian Heritage,* Feb., 1973, p. 28.

5. Sigmund Koch, "The Image of Man in Encounter Groups," in *The American Scholar,* Autumn, 1973 (Vol. 42, No. 4), p. 637.

6. *Christian Heritage,* Feb., 1973, pp. 28-29.

7. Sara Davidson, "The Rush for Instant Salvation," *Harpers,* July, 1971.

8. Moore, *The Young Adult Generation,* p. 128.

9. Gibson Winter, *Love and Conflict: New Patterns in Family Life* (Garden City, N.Y.: Doubleday and Co., 1958), p. 23.

10. David Stoop, "The Young Adult Population Boom and the Church," in *NADCE Digest,* Spring, 1973, p. 23.

11. *Ibid.*

12. Robert J. Havighurst, *Developmental Tasks and Education* (London: Longmans, Green, and Co., 1952).

13. Moore, *The Young Adult Generation,* p. 147.

14. *Ibid.*

CHAPTER 3:

1. J. Gordon Chamberlin, *The Church and Its Young Adults* (New York: Abingdon-Cokesbury, 1943), p. 15.

2. Elmer L. Towns, *Ministering to the Young Single Adult* (Grand Rapids, Mich.: Baker Book House, 1972), introduction, p. viii.

3. Harold D. Minor, *Techniques and Resources for Guiding Adult Groups* (Nashville: Abingdon Press, 1972), p. 15.

CHAPTER 4:

1. L. J. Bischof, *Adult Psychology* (New York: Harper and Row, Publishers, 1969), p. 4.

2. R. J. Havighurst, *Human Development and Education* (New York: Longman's, 1953), cited by E. B. Hurlock in *Development Psychology,* 4th ed. (New York: McGraw-Hill Book Co., 1975), p. 13.

3. R. J. Havighurst, *Developmental Tasks and Education,* 3rd ed. (New York: McKay, 1972), cited by R. E. Scheel, chief academic advisor and coordinator, *et al.,* in *Developmental Psy-*

chology Today, 2nd ed. (New York: Random House, Inc., 1975), pp. 412-13.

4. J. E. Birren, *The Psychology of Aging* (Englewood Cliffs, N.J.: Prentice-Hall, Inc., 1964), p. 6.

5. *Ibid.*

6. F. Franklyn Wise, "A Study of the Critical Requirements of Sunday Church School Teachers of Unmarried Youth of Certain Protestant Denominations" (Unpublished Ph.D. dissertation, School of Education, University of Pittsburgh, 1958).

7. Joann and Belden Menkus, "Adult Sunday School Needs to Grow Up," *Christianity Today* 19:15 (Apr. 24, 1975), p. 8.

Chapter 6:

1. John MacQuarrie, *Paths in Spirituality* (New York: Harper and Row, 1972), p. 55.

2. *Ibid.*

3. All of the theological issues are based on the 15 Articles of Faith in the Church of the Nazarene *Manual* (with the exception of No. 7 on the Church, which is prominent because of its absence). I would refer you to the new biblical theology, *God, Man, and Salvation* (Beacon Hill Press of Kansas City), which is in the process of publication as of this writing) and the *Manual,* Church of the Nazarene (Kansas City: Nazarene Publishing House, 1972). Cf. also H. Orton Wiley, *Christian Theology,* Vols. 1-3, (Kansas City: Beacon Hill Press, 1951-54) or H. Orton Wiley and Paul T. Culbertson, *Introduction to Christian Theology* (Kansas City: Beacon Hill Press, 1961).

4. Randolph Crump Miller, *Biblical Theology and Christian Education* (New York: Charles Scribner's Sons, 1956), p. 16.

5. *Ibid.*

6. Matt. 28:19-20; John 1:1-5, 14; 3:13; 8:58; 10:30; 14:9-10; 17:5, 24; Rom. 9:5; Phil. 2:5-11; 1 John 4:9; Rev. 1:8, 11; 21:6.

7. John 14:6, 26; Acts 5:3-4; 1 Cor. 12:6-11; 2 Cor. 3:17. A complete collation of scriptures concerning the personality of the Holy Spirit is given in Wiley, Vol. 1, p. 406.

8. James D. Smart, *The Creed in Christian Teaching* (Philadelphia: The Westminster Press, 1962), p. 183.

9. Gen. 1:27, 2:7; Ps. 8:3-4; Jer. 3:30; Ezek. 18:20; Matt. 23:

37; Rom. 1:20-21. Sin: Rom. 5:12; cf. also Ps. 51:5; 58:3; 1 Cor. 15:22; Wiley and Culbertson, ch. 10.

10. Isa. 53:4-5; John 3:16; Rom. 3:24-25; 5:6, 8, 11; 2 Cor. 5: 14-15, 18-19, 21; Eph. 5:2, 25; 1 Tim. 2:1-6; Heb. 2:9; 2 Pet. 3:9; cf. Wiley, 2:295-300. Holiness: Isa. 6:1-8; 35:8-10; Ezek. 36:25-28; Joel 2:28-32; Matt. 3:11-12; Mark 7:21-23; Luke 6:40; 11:9-13; 24: 49; John 14:15-18; 16:7-13; 17:3-16; Acts 1:4-8; 8:5-17; 9:17; 15:8- 9; 20:32; 26:15-18; Rom. 5:5; 6:11, 22; 8:1-2, 6-9; 12:1-2; 15:29; 1 Cor. 13; 2 Cor. 13:9; 1 Tim. 1:5; 2 Tim. 2:21; Heb. 2:11; 4:1-11; 6: 1-3; 10:10; 12:14-16; Jas. 4:8; 1 Pet. 1:15-16; 1 John 3:2-3; 4:17-18; Rev. 21:27; etc.

11. Heb. 10:24; cf. also Matt. 16:16-18; Acts 2:47; Romans 12; 1 Corinthians 12; Heb. 12:23; etc.

12. Smart, *Creed in Christian Teaching*, p. 217.

13. *Ibid.*, p. 195.

14. Key passages concerning the Church include "The Israel of God," Gal. 6:16; "God's building," 1 Cor. 3:5-9; "God's temple," 1 Cor. 3:16-17; cf. Prov. 2:9; Mark 10:43-45; John 14:1-8; Eph. 5:22-23; "Body of Christ," Rom. 12:4-8; 1 Cor. 12:12-27. See Harold DeWolf, *Responsible Freedom* (New York: Harper and Row, Pub., 1971), pp. 196-201, for an excellent discussion of the Church in an ethical perspective.

15. Matt. 26:64; Rom. 8:11; 1 Corinthians 15; 1 and 2 Thessalonians; Heb. 2:14-15; 9:28; Rev. 1:7; etc. See Wiley and Culbertson, pp. 401-45.

16. Smart, *Creed in Christian Teaching*, pp. 222-23.

17. *Ibid.*, p. 223.

CHAPTER 8:

1. Findley B. Edge, *Teaching for Results* (Nashville: Broadman Press, 1956), p. 1.

2. C. B. Eavey, *History of Christian Education* (Chicago: Moody Press, 1964), p. 77.

3. For further information on Jesus' use of questions and answers, see *The Teaching Methods of the Master*, by Claude C. Jones (St. Louis: The Bethany Press, 1957).

4. John 20:15. From the *New American Standard Bible*, copyright © The Lockman Foundation, 1960, 1962, 1963, 1968, 1971.

5. Jones, *Teaching Methods*, p. 33.

6. Edward Porter St. John, quoted by Jones, *ibid.*, p. 34.

7. John 15:5-6. From the *New American Standard Bible,* copyright © The Lockman Foundation, 1960, 1962, 1963, 1968, 1971.

8. Arnold Prater, *Release from Phoniness* (Waco: Word Books, 1969), p. 42.